Angular JS for Beginners: Your Guide to Easily Learn Angular JS in 7 Days

by

iCode Academy

Table of Contents

INTRODUCTION:

Welcome to this training for the Kindle version of the "AngularJS for Beginners: Your Guide to Easily Learn AngularJS Programming in 7 Days".

This book contains the steps, strategies, and techniques you need to learn and use AngularJS, a well-supported and widely-used JavaScript framework for single page applications development. This training material was conceptualized and developed to help beginners of diverse backgrounds to master the powerful features of AngularJS and use them to make rich and dynamic web pages.

Web developers, absolute beginners, and programmers will find this book a practical, engaging, and reliable resource material for learning AngularJS. Whether you want to launch a career in web applications development or you want to put up your own interactive website using the single page concept, this training offers a quick, straightforward, and inexpensive way to achieve your objectives.

This instructional book provides a thorough step-by-step guide to help you understand and optimize the tools, connectivity features, and potentials of AngularJS. It presents the precise steps from the beginning and discusses the key concepts involved in each step. It uses visual aids and screenshots to make learning intuitive and easy. This book offers a comprehensive discussion of AngularJS features and functionalities and provides real world examples that go beyond the basics.

Angular JS is a client-side Javascript framework that uses the MVC pattern to create dynamic web applications. It is an open-source framework that you can use to transform web pages from static to dynamic. It is completely based on HTML and Javascript so you don't need to learn another language or syntax. While knowledge of HTML, JavaScript, Ajax, and CSS can boost your learning speed, you can learn the basics of these languages and framework along with AngularJS.

The book "AngularJS for Beginners: Your Guide to Easily Learn AngularJS in 24 Hours" provides an intensive, definitive, and practical training to help you apply the many useful and stunning features of this easy-to-learn JavaScript framework as quickly as possible.

From setting the environment to launching your web applications, this book covers every step of the process. It will provide the information you need to access the functionalities and services that you can use to create truly dynamic and efficient web pages. You can learn AngularJS without spending more by using freely available and open source files, applications, language, and frameworks. You can use this environment to develop, test, and launch your web applications.

This book will help you acquire the skills and confidence you need to utilize the built-in features and capabilities of AngularJS. It provides tested examples that you can utilize to build your own dynamic single page application. It will empower you to design your own interactive web applications quickly and easily.

AngularJS offers numerous features that can help you create exciting web pages with a few lines of code. Many of these codes are reusable across different applications and within the current application. Learning the ins and outs of AngularJS will provide you with the skills that can help you create world class applications with less time and code.

AngularJS features several directives that you can use to work with data arrays, embed code from external HTML files, hide or show elements, and bind the AngularJS applications to HTML. These features allow you to set up client-side form validation controls, create dynamic tables, and display users' response in more exciting ways.

While it offers several built-in directives to make web applications development more efficient, AngularJS lets you create custom directives that you can use to implement unique concepts and applications that are more responsive to the needs of your website and users.

This book devotes one full chapter on Routing services which is the core concept of single page applications. This utility gives website users the experience of viewing a different page or functionality without navigating away from the current page. Learn this important concept using a step-by-step guide and example and enhance your web pages instantly.

AngularJS offers built-in filters that you can use to format output data and make them more readable and useful to viewers. This training material will show you how to make full use of these filters as well as how to create your own custom filters.

AngularJS has capabilities to perform client-side validation which helps ensure that viewers' input complies with the data format that a website form may require. Find out how you can use AngularJS, HTML, and JavaScript to implement a validation procedure on your registration page and in other areas of your website.

When you need to provide options for your dropdown lists, Angular offers a directive that you can use with the select option to create a dynamic list. This will allow you to use arrays or an object's key-value pairs as data source. Tapping the object as your source of data gives your application greater flexibility.

The book explores the many capabilities and possibilities of AngularJS. It presents each topic in a detailed yet straightforward way and demonstrates the concept with relevant, proven, and clear examples. It provides a detailed explanation for every important step in the process and displays the outcome through screenshots.

This training will equip you with the best practices and styles used by many web application developers. Taking this comprehensive training course on AngularJS will help you avoid costly mistakes that waste time and compromise productivity.

By the time you finish this book, you will have gained the confidence and technical skills to enhance your own website, create interactive web pages using the single page application concept, and use your web application development skills to create impressive web pages for commercial projects.

How long will it take you to learn AngularJS? With this book, you can learn AngularJS comfortably in a day or less. If you have strong HTML and Javascript background, you can easily acquire the important skills in a few hours.

Thank you for downloading this book. May you enjoy learning AngularJS and may it help you achieve your career and personal goals.

Chapter 1: ANGULAR JS – AN OVERVIEW

WHAT IS ANGULARJS?

AngularJS is a powerful open source JavaSript web framework backed by Google and a large supportive community of developers and programmers. It was created primarily to address the needs of single page applications development. It is used to create rich interactive features that make real-time experience possible. AngularJS extends HTML attributes and helps create more responsive applications that are easy to build and maintain.

ADVANTAGES OF USING ANGULARJS

AngularJS extends HTML capabilities and helps you create more powerful web applications. It provides its own elements called directives which serve as markers on DOM elements. This, in turn, instructs the compiler to bind a specific behavior to the HTML element.

AngularJS implements two-way binding and maintains data and view synchronization. It makes web development efficient by eliminating the need to create another JavaScript code to keep the data in HTML and the application data in sync. You will just have to specify in the same HTML code the control that will be attached to the specific part of the model.

AngularJS can handle routing, the process of moving between

views. Routing is the key concept behind single page applications. This allows the user to move between functionalities within the web application without leaving the current page.

AngularJS supports testing such as integration testing and unit testing.

It's an open source framework that's easy to download or access without downloading. It enjoys support from Google and a huge number of developers.

PREREQUISITES

To get the best out of this training, you should have a basic knowledge of JavaScript and HTML. Some knowledge of CSS, AJAX, and web applications will be very helpful.

If you have no prior knowledge of these web development languages, you can still try to learn them simultaneously with AngularJS.

ENVIRONMENT SETUP

In order to set up a development environment using AngularJS, you will need the following tools:

- AngularJS Library
- IDE/Editor
- Web server
- Browser

AngularJS Library

The AngularJS Library is free to download and use. To download, visit the Angularjs.org website. There are two options for download as this screenshot will show:

Click the Download AngularJS button and you'll see this popup:

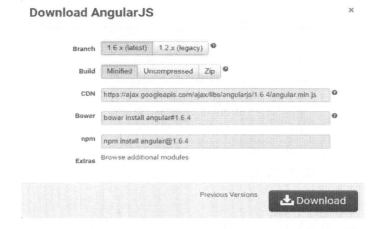

For this tutorial, choose to download the 1.6x latest version.

Alternatively, you may opt not to download the library and simply point the HTML <script></script> tag to a Google CDN URL. Most examples shown in this book uses the latter method.

You can point to one of two types of script URLs: angular.js and angular.min.js.

angular.js: This version is used for development.

angular.min.js: This minified version is used during production or when deploying your application.

You can use the following template to point your code to the minified version 1.6.4 on the Google CDN:

```html
<!doctype html>
<html ng-app>
 <head>
  <title>My AngularJS App</title>
  <script src="https://ajax.googleapis.com/ajax/libs/angularjs/1.6.4/angular.min.js"></script>
 </head>
 <body>
 </body>
</html>
```

IDE/Editor

AngularJS is practically a part of JavaScript and HTML code and you can work with any IDE or editor that will work well with both.

The following are the most commonly used IDE/editors:

Visual Studio
Net Beans
Eclipse
Sublime Text
Aptana Studio 3
Ultra Edit

You can also use Notepad for testing small pieces of code.

Web Server

You can use any web server such as Apache or IIS for development.

Browser

AngularJS is compatible with nearly all browsers but Google Chrome is the recommended browser while developing your applications.

MVC ARCHITECTURE

MVC stands for Model View Controller. It is a software design pattern that is widely used in web applications development. An MVC pattern consists of the following parts:

Model: The Model is responsible for maintaining data within the application. It is the lowest level of the design pattern. It interacts with the View and updates itself based on the instructions it receives from the Controller.

View: The View is the part that is responsible for presenting data to users. It refers to the display of data in a specific format dictated by the controller.

Controller: The Controller is the code that handles the interaction between the View and the Model. It responds to a user's input and interacts with data model objects. It receives and validates the input and performs operations that modify the Model.

The MVC is a widely used pattern because it supports the separation of concerns for the user interface layer and business/application logic. In this pattern, the controller handles all application requests and interacts with the Model to prepare the data required by the View. The View then generates a displayable response based on the data prepared by the Controller.

Here is a graphical presentation of the MVC software design pattern:

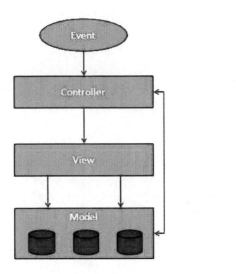

AngularJS is based on the MVC model. In succeeding chapters, you will see the MVC methodology at work in AngularJS web applications.

CHAPTER 2: CREATING A SIMPLE ANGULARJS APPLICATION

An AngularJS application has three important sections/directives:

ng-app: The ng-app directive defines an AngularJS application and links it to HTML.

ng-model: This directive binds application data to HTML controls(textarea, select, input).

ng-bind: This directive binds the application data to HTML view.

Using these three directives, you can easily create simple AngularJS applications. To create more useful applications, you will have to use the ng-controller directive. This directive accesses the controller which contains the logic of the application.

This simple application will demonstrate the building blocks of AngularJS:

Step 1: Create a basic HTML file containing the <head></head> and <body></body> elements:

```
<!DOCTYPE html>

<html>
<head>

</head>
<body>

</body>
</html>
```

Step 2: Add a reference to the AngularJS framework. It will tell AngularJS to start automatically when the web page has been loaded. You will do this within the <Script> tag:

```
<script
src="https://ajax.googleapis.com/ajax/libs/angularjs/1.6.4/angular.min.js">
</script>
```

Step 3: Use the ng-app directive to define the Angular application. You can give any name to the application but this example will define an application named myApp. On the same line, you will access the controller using the ng-controller directive. In this example, you will access the controller named "myCtrl" within the <div> tag. This controller contains the logic that will display the string "Hello, World!". The statement uses a member variable named "greeting" as a place holder for the message. Here's the statement:

```
<div ng-app="myApp" ng-controller="myCtrl">{{greeting}}
```

Step 4: Use the ng-model directive to define a model name:

```
Enter Your Name: <input type= text" ng-model="username"<br>
```

Step 5: Use the ng-bind directive to bind the value of the model:

```
<p>Good day, <span ng-bind = "name"></span>!</p>
```

Step 6: Use the 'var' keyword to create the AngularJS module named "MyApp":

```
var app = angular.module('myApp', []);
```

Step 7: Create the controller, the business logic of the application. In this example, you will build a controller and name it "myCtrl". On the same line, define a function with the $scope object as its parameter. The scope object is a global object that is used to handle the data between the view and the controller. This statement creates the controller named 'myCtrl' and defines a function that takes the $scope object as its parameter:

```
app.controller('myCtrl', function($scope) {
```

Step 8: Create a member variable and name it "greeting". Assign the string "Hello, World" to it and attach the member variable to the scope object. Here's the statement:

```
$scope.greeting = "Hello, World!";
```

You can put the above steps together to come up with your first AngularJS application. You can save the following as MyFirstApp:

```
<html>
    <script
src="https://ajax.googleapis.com/ajax/libs/angularjs/1.6.4/angular.min.js">
</script>
    <head>
        <title>MyFirstApp</title>
    </head>

    <body>
        <h1>My First Application</h1>

        <div ng-app="myApp" ng-controller="myCtrl">{{greeting}}
            <p>Enter your Name: <input type = "text" ng-model = "name"></p>
            <p>Hello <span ng-bind = "name"></span>!</p>
        </div>
            <script>
            var app = angular.module('myApp', []);
            app.controller('myCtrl', function($scope) {
            $scope.greeting = "Hello, World!";
            });
            </script>
    </body>
</html>
```

When you run the code, here's what the output might be:

If you try to enter the name Michelle on the textbox, here's what the browser will display:

Notice that the name 'Michelle' was also displayed on the last line.

AngularJS integration with HTML

The following summarizes how AngularJS integrates with HTML:

The ng-app directive marks the beginning of an Angular application within an HTML document.

The ng-model directive is used to create a model variable. This is used inside the <div> tag containing the ng-app directive and within an HTML page.

The ng-bind directive attaches the model name to HTML view through the span tag and causes the display of a user's input in the text box.

The closing </div> tag marks the termination of an AngularJS application.

CHAPTER 3: CONTROLLERS

AngularJS applications depend on controllers to manage data flow. A controller is a Javascript object that contains the core business logic of an application. It takes the data from the View, performs the required processes, and sends the data to the View which, in turn, is displayed to end users.

FUNCTIONS OF A CONTROLLER

The primary function of a controller is to manage the data that gets passed to the View. There is a two-way communication between the view and the scope. This relationship is illustrated by this diagram:

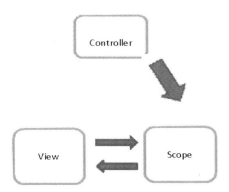

The events on the View can call the methods while its properties can call the functions defined on the scope.

The following section of a code shows an example of an AngularJS function and method:

```
app.controller('personCtrl', function($scope) {
   $scope.firstName = "John";
   $scope.lastName = "Doe";
   $scope.fullName = function() {
      return $scope.firstName + " " + $scope.lastName;
   };
```

The function ($scope), three variables, and an internal function () were defined when the controller 'personCtrl' was created. The internal function outputs a concatenation of the member variables $scope.firstName and $scope.lastName. In AngularJS, a function defined as a variable is called a method.

This structure allows the transmission of data from the controller to the $scope which triggers the two-way exchange between the $scope and the View. The $scope renders the model to the View. It can modify the model using methods defined inside the $scope when triggered by events in the View.

It is a common industry practice to create a controller based on functionality and to give it a name that describes what it does. For instance, if you need a controller to handle form input, you can create a controller and call it 'form controller'.

BUILDING A CONTROLLER

AngularJS applications depend on controllers to manage data flow. A controller is a Javascript object that contains properties and functions. It takes $scope as an argument. The argument, in turn, points to the module/application that the controller handles.

The ng-controller directive is used to define a controller. Before you can start creating a controller, you have to create a basic HTML page.

The following code section shows an HTML file with references to Angular, jquery, and bootstrap libraries:

```
<!DOCTYPE html>
<html>
    <head>
        <title>Global Events Management</title>
        <meta charset="UTF-8">
        <link rel="stylesheet" href="css.bootstrap.css">
    </head>
    <body>
        <h1>Worldwide Cultural Events</h1>
        <script src="lib/angular.js"></script>
        <script src="lib/bootstrap.js"></script>
        <script src="lib/jquery-1.11.3.min.js"></script>
```

References were added to the bootstrap CSS style sheets, angularjs libraries, bootstrap, and jquery libraries for the following purposes:

bootstrap CSS stylesheets: These will be needed to complement the bootstrap libraries.

angularjs library: This will be used to reference anything that has to do with the AngularJS script. You will have to include this in your script if you've chosen to download AngularJS on your computer. Otherwise, you can simply make a reference to the Google CDN as explained in Chapter 1.

bootstrap library: Reference to this library will allow web pages to become more responsive to certain controls.

jquery library: Some Angular functionalities depend on the jquery properties for DOM manipulation so a reference to this library might be required by your application.

File Structure

As commonly done with most web applications, the files are separated into two folders: the CSS folder and the 'lib' folder.

All cascading style sheet files are stored in the CSS folder. The bootstrap.css file is likewise saved in this folder.

The 'lib' folder will contain all Javascript files. If you have opted to download from the AngularJS.org site, the angular.js file will be stored inside the 'lib' folder. The apps.js file will be used to store the codes for your controllers. The jquery file lets you use certain DOM manipulation functionalities. The bootstrap.js file adds bootstrap features to your application and supplements the bootstrap.css file.

The following is a simple AngularJS program that will display the string "Global Trade Show" as a text inside a text box:

```
<div ng-app="EventApp" ng-controller="EventController">
    Event Title: <input type="text" ng-model="eventName"><br>
    <br>
    The Event is {{eventName}}
</div>
<script type="text/javascript">
    var app = angular.module('EventApp', []);
    app.controller('EventController', function($scope) {
        $scope.eventName = "Global Trade Show";
        })
</script>
```

Here are the key points of the code:

The ng-app keyword indicates that the application is an AngularJS application. Bear in mind that in AngularJS, a keyword with an 'ng' prefix is a directive. The name of the AngularJS application is EventApp.

The code uses a <div> tag to which an ng-controller directive was added. The controller was named EventController. The name of the controller has to be given within the directive to enable the application to access the controller's functionality. This allows the <div> tag to access the functionality defined inside the EventController.

The ng-model directive is used to establish model binding. In this case, it attaches the textbox for Event Name to the member variable "eventName".

The application creates a member variable named 'eventName". This variable will be used to show what the user will type in the textbox beside the Event Name.

The code likewise creates a module that will be linked to the EventApp application. This module contains a function definition that gives a default value to the variable eventName.

If you run the code, here's what the output might be:

Worldwide Cultural Events

Event Title: Global Trade Show

The Event is Global Trade Show

CONTROLLER METHODS

In AngularJS, it is a common practice to create several methods in a controller. This supports separation of business logic within the application.

For instance, assuming that you want a controller to perform two operations such as multiplication and division, you would prefer to define two methods within a controller. One method will do the multiplication while the other will do the division.

You can, in fact, create custom methods inside AngularJS controllers. This example will demonstrate how this can be done in AngularJS:

```html
<!DOCTYPE html>
<html>
    <head>
        <title>Global Events Management</title>
        <meta charset="UTF-8">
        <link rel="stylesheet" href="css.bootstrap.css">
        <script
            src="https://ajax.googleapis.com/ajax/libs/angularjs/1.6.4/angular.min.js">
        </script>
    </head>
    <body>
        <h1>Worldwide Cultural Events</h1>
        <script src="lib/bootstrap.js"></script>
        <script src="lib/jquery-1.11.3.min.js"></script>
        <div ng-app="eventApp" ng-controller="eventController">
            Event Title: <input type = "text" ng-model = "eventName()"><br>
            <br>
            The Event is {{eventName()}};
        </div>
        <script type="text/javascript">
            var app = angular.module('eventApp', []);
            app.controller('eventController', function($scope) {
                $scope.eventName = function() {
                    return "Global Trade Show"
                };
            });
        </script>
    </body>
</html>
```

The above example defines a function which returns the string "Global Trade Show". It is linked to the $scope object through the member variable named 'eventName'.

When you execute the code in your browser, here's what the output should be:

CONTROLLERS IN EXTERNAL FILES

So far, you have seen codes where all functionalities were placed in one file. In this section, you will learn how to store and access the controller in a separate file.

To do this, you can follow the following steps:

Step 1: Add this code for the controller in the app.js file:

```
<div ng-app = "">
    ...
</div>
angular.module('app',[]).controller('GreetingsCtrl',
    function($scope)
    {
        scope.greeting="Hello, World!"
})
```

The code performs the following tasks:

- It defines a module named 'app' which contains the controller and its functionality.
- It creates a controller called "GreetingsCtrl". This controller will have a functionality of displaying the "Hello, World!" greeting.

The controller's $scope object passes data from the "GreetingsCtrl" to the view. In this example, it is used to contain a variable named "greeting".

The code defines the "greeting" variable and assigns the value "Hello, World!" to this variable.

Step 2: In the HTML file, add a <div> class. This will hold the ng-controller directive and provide reference to the "greeting" variable. Likewise, include a reference to the app.js script file which contains the "GreetingsCtrl" source code.

Here's the code:

```
<!DOCTYPE html>
<html ng-app=app>
    <head>
        <title>Global Events Management</title>
        <meta charset="UTF-8">
        <link rel="stylesheet" href="css.bootstrap.css">
    </head>
    <body>
        <h1>Worldwide Cultural Events</h1>
        <div class="container">
            <div ng-controller="GreetingsCtrl">{{greeting}}</div>
        </div>
        <script src="lib/angular.js"></script>
        <script src="lib/bootstrap.js"></script>
        <script src="lib/jquery-1.11.3.min.js"></script>
        <script src="lib/app.js"></script>
    </body>
</html>
```

If you run the code, this will be your output:

MANAGING SCOPE

The scope is used to bind the Controller and the View. A JavaScript object, the scope contains the model data and has methods and properties that can be accessed by both the View and the Controller. To use the scope, you have to pass the $scope object as an argument in the controller. You can define member variables through the scope object inside the Controller. In turn, the View will be able to access these variables.

Study the following script:

```
angular.module('app',[]).controller('GreetingsCtrl',
    function($scope)
    {
        $scope.greeting="Hello, World!"
        $scope.name="ABC World"
        $scope.version="BC-2"
    })
```

The script tells us that the $scope object can be used to define one or more member variables that can hold useful values.

You can display these values using the <div> tag. This further demonstrates that the scope object is the main medium used by the Controller for passing data to the View.

ADDING BEHAVIOR

For your application to respond to events or perform the processing you need in the View, you have to add behavior to the $scope. Behaviors allow $scope objects to react to particular events that the View may trigger. Defining a behavior within the controller enables the View to access that behavior.

This example will demonstrate how you can do this:

```
<!DOCTYPE html>
<html>
<script
src="https://ajax.googleapis.com/ajax/libs/angularjs/1.6.4/angular.min.js">
</script>
<body>

<div ng-app="myApp" ng-controller="demoCtrl">

{{fullName("John", "Swish")}}

</div>

<script>
var app = angular.module('myApp', []);
app.controller('demoCtrl', function($scope) {
    $scope.fullName = function(firstName, lastName) {
        return firstName + " " + lastName;
    }
});
</script>

</body>
</html>
```

The code creates a behavior named "fullName". It is a function that takes 2 arguments, firstName, and lastName. This behavior returns a concatenation of these two arguments. The behavior will be called in the View and the values "John" and "Swish" will be passed as arguments to this behavior.

When you run the code, here's what will appear on the browser:

DISPLAYING REPEATED BEHAVIOR

In some cases, you may need to show multiple items in the View.

The ng-repeat directive is used to show repeating values defined within the controller.

This example will show how you can do this in AngularJS:

```
<!DOCTYPE html>
<html>
<script
src="https://ajax.googleapis.com/ajax/libs/angularjs/1.6.4/angular.min.js">
</script>
<body>
<hi>Topics</h1>
<div ng-app="myApp" ng-controller="myCtrl">
    <ul><li ng-repeat="tname in topics.topicNames">
        {{tname.name}}
    </li></ul>
</div>

<script type="text/javascript">
var app = angular.module('myApp', []);
app.controller('myCtrl', function($scope) {
    $scope.topics=
    {
        topicNames : [
        {name: "Structure of Web Page"},
        {name: "Dynamic Web Pages"},
        {name: "Extending HTML Attributes"}]}});
</script>
</body>
</html>
```

Here are the key points of the code:

The application first defines an array of items in the controller. The code defines an array named topicNames which contains three key-value pairs.

This array was added to the member variable named "topics" and linked to the $scope object.

It uses the <ul> HTML tags to show the list of array items.

The ng-repeat directive is then used to go through all the items of the array. The variable "tname" was used to point to every item in the topics.topicNames array.

When you run the code on the browser, this will be the result:

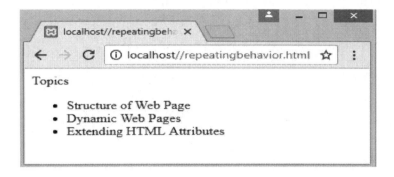

Notice that it displayed all items in the array.

CREATING AN ADVANCED CONTROLLER

So far, you have seen simple codes which use a single controller. In AngularJS, having multiple controllers in an application is an example of creating advanced controllers.

Creating multiple controllers within an application is ideal for separating business logic functions and creating a more efficient and cleaner code. For instance, you can create a controller which performs operation on strings and another controller which will handle operations on numbers.

In this section, you will see how you can create several controllers to achieve a higher level of logic separation.

The following is a simple code that will create two controllers:

```
<!DOCTYPE html>
<html>
<script
src="https://ajax.googleapis.com/ajax/libs/angularjs/1.6.4/angular.min.js">
</script>
<body>
<div ng-app="myApp">
<div ng-controller="firstCtrl">
<div ng-controller="secondCtrl">
    {{pname}}
</div>
</div>
</div>
<script>
var app = angular.module('myApp', []);
app.controller('firstCtrl', function($scope) {
    $scope.lname="firstCtrl";
});
app.controller('secondCtrl', function($scope) {
    $scope.pname="secondCtrl";
});
</script>
</body>
</html>
```

The code defines two controllers named 'firstCtrl' and 'secondCtrl'. The variable named 'lname' with a value of 'firstCtrl' was attached to the 'firstCtrl' while the variable named 'pname' with a value of 'secondCtrl' was attached to the 'secondCtrl'.

You will access the two controllers and output the member variable of the 'secondCtrl' in the view.

When you execute the code, this will be the output.

As you would expect, the web browser displayed the text value of the second controller.

Summary:

The primary function of a controller is to create a scope object that will be passed to the View.

You can create a simple controller by using the ng-app, ng-model, and ng-controller directives.

Custom methods may be added to a controller to separate functionalities within a module.

Defining controllers in external files is considered one of the best practices in web applications development. This separates the logic layer from the View layer and makes the code cleaner and more efficient.

You can add several member variables to the $scope object and make them accessible to the View.

Behaviors may be added to the $scope object to enable them to respond to events generated by the user's action.

You can use the ng-repeat directive to display repeating items defined within the controller.

An application can have multiple controllers.

CHAPTER 4: VIEWS

In the concept of "Single Page Applications" (SPA), the application does not navigate to the page requested by a user but displays the view of the requested page within the current page. This gives the impression that the user did not leave the current page at all. You can achieve this in AngularJS by combining Views with Routes.

The View refers to the model's projection through an HTML template. AngularJS refreshes the corresponding binding points whenever it detects a change in the model. This, in turn, will update the view. Basically, a view is the content that is displayed to the user in response to the user's request.

Views, in conjunction with Routes, facilitate the logical division of an application into different views. This makes the application more manageable.

AngularJS provides the $routeProvider service as well as the ng-view and ng-templates directives to allow multiple views on a single page.

For example, in a typical ordering application, a user can view his/her existing order and place new orders. The following diagram illustrates how you can turn this application into an SPA:

OrderApp/#show →	View Orders	Controller - View Orders
OrderApp/#new →	New Orders	Controller - New Orders

The diagram indicates that two different views were created, namely, "View Orders" and "New Orders" and they are displayed on the same page.

Notice the reference links called #show and #new. Whenever the application is directed to the OrderApp/#show, it displays the View Orders view but does not navigate away from the page. It simply refreshes the current page with data from "View Orders". The same thing happens when the application goes to the OrderApp/#new. It will refresh the current page and display information from "New Orders".

When the application is separated into different views, it is easier to make changes when needed. In addition, each view is given a controller that will handle the business logic for its functionality. The application thus becomes more manageable.

AngularJs Views

The ng-view directive works with the ngRoute module by including the current route's template into the index.html or main layout file. Each time there is a change in the current route, the view includes the changes based on the $route service configuration without reloading the page.

This chapter will focus on Views. Routing will be discussed further in another chapter.

In the following example, the web page will display two choices to the user: 'View Employees' and 'Add an Employee'. When a user clicks on the 'View Employees' link, the application will display the view for 'View Employees'. In the same way, when a user clicks on the link for 'Add an Employee', the application will show the view for 'Add an Employee'.

To implement the Single Page Application concept, you need to perform the following steps:

Step 1: Include the Angular Route module in the script reference.

```
<script src="https://ajax.googleapis.com/ajax/libs/angularjs/1.6.4/angular-route.js"></script>
```

You will need the Route module to access the functionalities of multiple views and routes. The AngularJS route module, in turn, will provide the $routeProvider. You will use this service to set up the different routes in your application.

Step 2: Add href tags to represent the links to the options "View Employees" and "Add an Employee".

In addition, you need to include an ng-view directive within the <div> tag to represent the view. This will inject the corresponding view when a user opts to click on either the "View Employees" or "Add an Employee" link.

The following code adds href tags and the ng-view directive:

```
<div ng-app = "mainApp">
    <p><a href = "#!addEmployee">Add an Employee</a></p>
    <p><a href = "#!viewEmployees">View Employees</a></p>
    <div ng-view=""></div>
```

Step 3: Include ngRoute as a dependency in your application module:

```
var app = angular.module("mainApp", ['ngRoute']);
```

Step 4: Add the following code within the AngularJS script tag:

```
app.config(function($routeProvider) {
    $routeProvider
     .when('/addEmployee', {
       templateUrl: 'addEmployee.html',
       controller: 'AddEmployeeController'
     })
     .when('/viewEmployees', {
       templateUrl: 'viewEmployees.html',
       controller: 'ViewEmployeesController'
     })
     .otherwise({
       redirectTo: '/addEmployee'
     });
    });

    app.controller('AddEmployeeController', function($scope) {
      $scope.message = "This page will display the Add Employee form";
    });

    app.controller('ViewEmployeesController', function($scope) {
      $scope.message = "This page will display the list of employees";
    });
```

The succeeding paragraphs will discuss the important sections of the above code:

The code snippet below indicates that when a user clicks on the href tag 'addEmployee', the application will be directed to and will take the code from the addEmployee.html template. It will then use the template to display the data in the View. Take note that the addEmployee tag was defined earlier in the <div> tag. In addition, the code processes the business logic for the corresponding view by directing the application to the 'AddEmployeeController'.

```
.when('/addEmployee', {
        templateUrl: 'addEmployee.html',
        controller: 'AddEmployeeController'
})
```

The following code section means that when a user clicks on the href tag 'viewEmployees', the application will be directed to and will take the code from the viewEmployees.html template and inject it in the View. Like the addEmployee tag, the viewEmployees tag was defined earlier in the <div> tag. Additionally, the application handles the business logic for this view by directing the application to the 'viewEmployeesController'.

```
.when('/viewEmployees', {
        templateUrl:
'viewEmployees.html',
        controller:
'ViewEmployeesController'
})
```

This section indicates that the addEmployees view is the default view for the application:

```
.otherwise({
        redirectTo: '/addEmployee'
});
```

Step 5: Add controllers to handle the business logic for the 'Add an Employee' and 'View Employees' functionalities.

In this section, you will add a message variable to the scope object of the AddEmployeeController and ViewEmployeesController. The message will be shown when the corresponding view is displayed to the user:

```
app.controller('AddEmployeeController', function($scope) {
     $scope.message = "This page will display the Add Employee form";
     });

     app.controller('ViewEmployeesController', function($scope) {
       $scope.message = "This page will display the list of employees";
     });
```

Step 6: Create two web pages and save them as 'addEmployee.html' and 'viewEmployees.html'.

In this example, the addEmployee webpage will contain a header tag with the string "Add an Employee" and will display the message "This page will display the Add Employee form".

Likewise, the viewEmployees webpage will also include a header tag with the string "View Employees" and will show the message "This page will display the list of employees".

The value assigned to the message variable will be displayed based on the controller attached to the requested view. Hence, for addEmployee and viewEmployees pages, you will need to include the message variable from their corresponding controller.

For the addEmployee.html, the code can be as simple as this:

```
<h2>Add an Employee</h2>
{{message}}
```

The scope variable of the AddEmployees controller will be injected into the message expression of the above template.

For the viewEmployees.html, you can use this code:

```
<h2>View Employees</h2>
{{message}}
```

The scope variable of the ViewEmployees controller will be injected into the message expression of the above viewEmployees.html template.

If you string together these snippets into one coherent code, here's how it may appear:

```html
<html>
    <head>
        <title>Angular JS Views</title>
        <script src =
"https://ajax.googleapis.com/ajax/libs/angularjs/1.6.4/angular.min.js">
</script>
        <script src =
"https://ajax.googleapis.com/ajax/libs/angularjs/1.6.4/angular-route.min.js">
</script>
    </head>

    <body>
        <h2>AngularJS Application</h2>
        <div ng-app = "mainApp">
            <p><a href = "#!addEmployee">Add an Employee</a></p>
            <p><a href = "#!viewEmployees">View Employees</a></p>
            <div ng-view=""></div>

            <script type = "text/ng-template" id = "addEmployee.html">
                <h2> Add an Employee </h2>
                {{message}}
            </script>

            <script type = "text/ng-template" id = "viewEmployees.html">
                <h2> View Employees </h2>
                {{message}}
            </script>
        </div>

        <script>
        var app = angular.module("mainApp", ['ngRoute']);
        app.config(function($routeProvider) {
            $routeProvider
                .when('/addEmployee', {
                    templateUrl: 'addEmployee.html',
                    controller: 'AddEmployeeController'
                })
                .when('/viewEmployees', {
                    templateUrl: 'viewEmployees.html',
                    controller: 'ViewEmployeesController'
                })
                .otherwise({
                    redirectTo: '/addEmployee'
                });
        });

        app.controller('AddEmployeeController', function($scope) {
            $scope.message = "This page will display the Add Employee form";
        });

        app.controller('ViewEmployeesController', function($scope) {
            $scope.message = "This page will display the list of employees";
        });
        </script>
    </body>
</html>
```

When you run the code, this is what the browser will display:

AngularJS Application

Add an Employee

View Employees

Add an Employee

This page will display the Add Employee form

From the above result, we can deduce the following:

The address bar reflects the active view that the user had requested to be displayed. Since the code specified the addEmployee view as the default view, the address bar displays the address for 'addEmployee'.

The View which shows 'Add an Employee' is the default view displayed to the users.

If you click on the 'View Employees' link, the browser will display this page:

AngularJS Application

Add an Employee

View Employees

View Employees

This page will display the list of employees

The address bar now reflects the 'viewEmployees' route. Take note that the user is not directed to another application page but stays on the same page. The View shows 'View Employees'.

Ng-view directive

The ng-view directive is used to create a place holder where you can place a corresponding view according to its configuration. To use it, you will define a <div> that contains an ng-view inside the main module.

Here's an example:

```
<div ng-app = "mainApp">
  ...
  <div ng-view></div>
</div>
```

Ng-template directive

This directive is used to create HTML views using script tags. The $routeProvider uses its 'id' attribute to map a view through a controller. To use the $ng-template directive, a script block with ng-template type is defined inside the main module.

Here's an example:

```
<div ng-app = "mainApp">
  ...

  <script type = "text/ng-template" id = "addEmployees.htm">
    <h2> Add Employee </h2>
    {{message}}
  </script>

</div>
```

$routeProvider

The $routeProvider sets the configuration of URLs, map them with a corresponding ng-template or html page, and bind a controller to them. To use the $routeProvider, you will need to define a script inside the main module and set its routing configuration.

Here's an example:

```
var app = angular.module("mainApp", ['ngRoute']);
app.config(function($routeProvider) {
    $routeProvider
        .when('/addEmployee', {
            templateUrl: 'addEmployee.html',
            controller: 'AddEmployeeController'
        })
        .when('/viewEmployees', {
            templateUrl: 'viewEmployees.html',
            controller: 'ViewEmployeesController'
        })
        .otherwise({
            redirectTo: '/addEmployee'
        });
});
```

Take note of the following key points:

The $routeProvider was designated as a function within the configuration of the mainApp module.

The $routeProvider.when defines an '/addEmployees' URL and maps it to "addEmployees.html". Make sure that the addEmployees.html file is stored in the path that contains the main HTML page. If the page is not defined, the ng-template will be used with id="addEmployees.html".

The 'otherwise' method sets the default view.

The 'controller' method sets the controller for the view.

Chapter 5: DIRECTIVES

Directives are attributes or markers that attach a specific behavior to an HTML element. These attributes are used to extend HTML. AngularJS offers several built-in directives that provide functionality to web applications. These directives typically start with the ng- prefix. You can also define your own set of directives.

This chapter will discuss the most commonly used AngularJS directives and show how you can create and invoke new directives.

BUILT-IN DIRECTIVES

Ng-app directive

This directive is the starting point of AngularJS applications. Whenever the AngularJS framework encounters the ng-app directive in an HTML documents, it automatically initializes or bootstraps itself and compiles the HTML template. This directive indicates to AngularJS framework that the specific <div> element 'owns' the application. The ng-app directive is likewise used to load AngularJS modules inside AngularJS applications.

Ng-init directive

This directive initializes AngularJS application data. This is what you will use to assign values to the variables that will be used in your application.

Ng-model

The ng-model directive attaches the values of application data to HTML controls (textarea, select, input). It is used to bind an HTML element to an attribute on the $scope object. It can also provide application data type validation and attach HTML forms to HTML elements. The ng-model can be used to indicate the status of application data (error, touched, invalid, dirty) and give CSS classes for HTML elements.

Ng-repeat directive

This directive repeats or clones html elements for every item in a collection.

CREATING AND INVOKING CUSTOM DIRECTIVES

In addition to providing several directives, AngularJS allows you to create your own directives using the .directive function. To invoke this directive, you will have to create an HTML element that will have the same tag name as the newly created directive.

The camel case name convention is used when naming a directive. For example, you may create a directive by naming it as newSampleDirective. However, to invoke the new directive, you will use the hyphenated name. For example, to invoke the newSampleDirective, you will refer to it as new-sample-directive.

The following example creates a new directive named createNewDirective by creating a new HTML element named create-new-directive:

```
<!DOCTYPE html>
<html>
<script src="https://ajax.googleapis.com/ajax/libs/angularjs/1.6.4/angular.min.js"></script>
<body ng-app="myApp">

<create-new-directive></create-new-directive>

<script>
var app = angular.module("myApp", []);
app.directive("createNewDirective", function() {
    return {
        template : "<h1>Generated by a new directive!</h1>"
    };
});
</script>
</body>
</html>
```

If you execute the code, the output would be:

The above example invoked a directive using the HTML element <create-new-directive>. You can also invoke a directive using any of the following to come up with the same output:

Attribute
Class
Comment

The following example uses an HTML attribute to invoke the new directive:

```
<!DOCTYPE html>
<html>
<script src="https://ajax.googleapis.com/ajax/libs/angularjs/1.6.4/angular.min.js"></script>
<body ng-app="myApp">

<div create-new-directive></div>

<script>
var app = angular.module("myApp", []);
app.directive("createNewDirective", function() {
   return {
      template : "<h1>Generated by a new directive!</h1>"
   };
});
</script>
</body>
</html>
```

Here's the result:

This examples uses class to invoke the new directive:

```
<!DOCTYPE html>
<html>
<script src="https://ajax.googleapis.com/ajax/libs/angularjs/1.6.4/angular.min.js"></script>
<body ng-app="myApp">

<div class="create-new-directive"></div>

<script>
var app = angular.module("myApp", []);
app.directive("createNewDirective", function() {
   return {
      restrict : "C",
      template : "<h1>Generated by a new directive!</h1>"
   };
});
</script>
</body>
</html>
```

Notice that the value "C" was assigned to the restrict property. This allows the new directive to be called from a class.

The output would be:

The following example uses a 'comment' to invoke the new directive:

```
<!DOCTYPE html>
<html>
<script src="https://ajax.googleapis.com/ajax/libs/angularjs/1.6.4/angular.min.js"></script>
<body ng-app="myApp">

<!-- directive: create-new-directive -->

<script>
var app = angular.module("myApp", []);
app.directive("createNewDirective", function() {
    return {
        restrict : "M",
        replace : true,
        template : "<h1>Generated by a new directive!</h1>"
    };
});
</script>
</body>
</html>
```

Take note that the 'restrict' and 'replace' properties were added within the return block.

The value "M" was assigned to the restrict property to allow the directive to be called from a comment.

The replace property was added to make the comment visible.

When you run the code, here's what the output will be:

Restrictions

You can place restriction on your directives to limit the methods that can be used to invoke them.

For example, if you want a directive to be invoked only by attributes, you can assign the value "A" to the restrict property. Here's an example:

```
<!DOCTYPE html>
<html>
<script src="https://ajax.googleapis.com/ajax/libs/angularjs/1.6.4/angular.min.js"></script>
<body ng-app="myApp">

<create-new-directive></create-new-directive>

<div create-new-directive></div>


<script>
var app = angular.module("myApp", []);
app.directive("createNewDirective", function() {
   return {
      restrict : "A",
      template : "<h1>Generated by a new directive!</h1>"
   };
});
</script>
</body>
</html>
```

Notice that the code provides two methods to invoke the new directive: the HTML element and attribute methods. However, since the value of "A" was assigned to the restrict property, only the attribute method can be used to invoke the directive.

You can use the following legal restrict values to impose restrictions:

A   Attribute
E   Element name
M   Comment
C   Class

The default value is EA which means that you can use both Attribute and Element names to call the directive.

CHAPTER 6: DATA BINDING

In AngularjJS, data binding refers to the synchronization between the view and the model. A data model refers to a collection of data that you can access in an application. Most AngularJS applications have a data model.

HTML View

The View is the HTML container that will display the data in an AngularJS application. The model is accessible to the view and there are different options for showing the model's data in the view.

One option is to use the ng-bind directive. This directive binds the element's innerHTML to a defined model attribute.

The following example binds the innerHTML element to the firstname attribute of the model:

<p ng-bind="firstname"></p>

```
<!DOCTYPE html>
<html>
<script src="https://ajax.googleapis.com/ajax/libs/angularjs/1.6.4/angular.min.js"></script>
<body>

<div ng-app="newApp" ng-controller="myController">
   <p ng-bind="firstname"></p>
</div>

<script>
var app = angular.module('newApp', []);
app.controller('myController', function($scope) {
   $scope.firstname = "Michael";
   $scope.lastname = "Dawning";
});
</script>
<p>Uses the ng-bind directive to attach an element's innerHTML to an attribute in the data model.</p>
</body>
</html>
```

When you run the code, it will produce the following result:

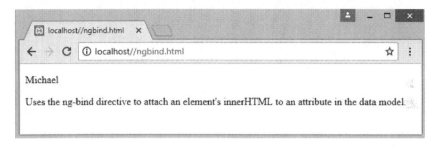

Another option for displaying data from the model is by using double braces {{ }}.

The following example will use basically the same data in the previous example except that a string will be used in place of the ng-bind and the model property that will be displayed, firstname, is placed inside the double braces:

```
<!DOCTYPE html>
<html>
<script src="https://ajax.googleapis.com/ajax/libs/angularjs/1.6.4/angular.min.js"></script>
<body>

<div ng-app="newApp" ng-controller="myController">
   <p>First name: {{firstname}}</p>
</div>

<script>
var app = angular.module('newApp', []);
app.controller('myController', function($scope) {
   $scope.firstname = "Michael";
   $scope.lastname = "Dawning";
});
</script>

<p>You can use double braces to display a specified content from the model.</p>

</body>
</html>
```

When you execute the code, here's what the result would be:

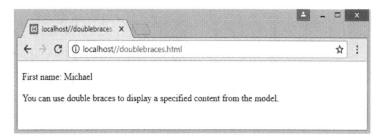

Likewise, the ng-model directive may be used on HTML controls (textarea, select, input) to attach a model's element to the view. In this code snippet, for example, the HTML control element 'input' is used with ng-model to bind the "firstname" element of the model to the view:

<input ng-model="firstname">

Here's a simple code that demonstrates the use of ng-model on the input element to bind the model property "firstname".

```
<!DOCTYPE html>
<html>
<script src="https://ajax.googleapis.com/ajax/libs/angularjs/1.6.4/angular.min.js"></script>
<body>

<div ng-app="newApp" ng-controller="myController">
   <input ng-model="firstname">
</div>

<script>
var app = angular.module('newApp', []);
app.controller('myController', function($scope) {
   $scope.firstname = "Michael";
   $scope.lastname = "Dawning";
});
</script>

<p>You can use the ng-model directive on HTML controls (textarea, input, select)
to bind data between the view and the model.</p>

</body>
</html>
```

If you run the above code, it will produce the following result:

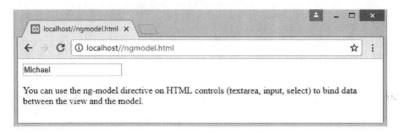

TWO-WAY BINDING

Data binding refers to the synchronization between the view and the model. The use of the ng-model directive facilitates this two-way binding. This means that changes in the model's data is reflected in the view and that changes in the view updates the model as well. This two-way updating happens automatically and instantly which ensures that both are always updated.

The following example demonstrates the two-way binding between the model and the view:

```
<!DOCTYPE html>
<html>
<script src="https://ajax.googleapis.com/ajax/libs/angularjs/1.6.4/angular.min.js"></script>
<body>

<div ng-app="newApp" ng-controller="myController">
    First Name: <input ng-model="firstname">
    <h1>{{firstname}}</h1>
</div>

<script>
var app = angular.module('newApp', []);
app.controller('myController', function($scope) {
    $scope.firstname = "Michael";
    $scope.lastname = "Dawning";
});
</script>
```

When you the code, it will show the following output:

First Name: Michael

Michael

If you try to enter a different name, say 'Kurt', the header will automatically change to reflect the current data. Here's the output:

First Name: Kurt |

Kurt

CHAPTER 7: EXPRESSIONS

An expression is used to attach application data to HTML. Expressions are wrapped inside double curly braces like {{8 + 4}}. They may also be written inside a directive like ng-bind="expression". AngularJS expressions behave like the ng-bind directive when they are used to bind data to HTML. AngularJS applications are practically JavaScript codes where the AngularJS resolves the expression and displays the data where the expression is written.

Like JavaScript expression, AngularJS expressions can contain variables, operators, objects, arrays, and literals.

Examples

```
{{10 x 2 }}
{{ FName + " " + LName }}
<p>Ticket Expense : {{quantity * ucost}} Rs</p>
<p>Roll Number: {{student.rollnum}}</p>
<p>Marks(Science): {{marks[4]}}</p>
```

Capabilities of AngularJS Expressions

AngularJS expressions have the same power and flexibility as that of JavaScript expressions.

AngularJS expressions are more forgiving than Javascript expressions. For instance, when evaluating undefined properties, JavaScript will generate a TypeError or ReferenceError while AngularJS will simply return undefined or null.

AngularJS lets you use filters inside the expressions. This facilitates formatting of data prior to presentation.

Limitations of Angular JS Expressions

Presently, you can't use exceptions, loops, or conditional statements in AngularJS expressions.

You can't create regular expressions within an AngularJS expression. A regular expression consists of a combination of characters and symbols that can be used to search for strings like '*/run$'.

AngularJS will not allow you to declare functions within an expression.

The following example will show a simple expression using the multiplication operation:

```
<!doctype html>
<html ng-app>
 <head>
  <title>AngularJS Expressions</title>
  <script src="https://ajax.googleapis.com/ajax/libs/angularjs/1.6.4/angular.min.js"></script>
 </head>
 <body>
 <h1>Multiplication Operation</h1>
   <div ng-app="">
   Multiplication
   {{3*5}}
 </body>
</html>
```

Notice that in this code, the ng-app directive is blank and not set to any application name. Hence, there would be no module to assign controllers or directives. The expression applies the multiplication operator between two numbers and is enclosed in double curly braces.

When you execute the code in the browser, you might see something like this:

Based on the above result, you can conclude that the multiplication operation was performed on the numbers 3 and 5 and that the result of the operation was displayed.

USING EXPRESSIONS WITH NUMBER VARIABLES

The following code will demonstrate the addition of two number variables named labor and materials and show the total value:

```
<!doctype html>
<html ng-app>
 <head>
  <title>AngularJS Expressions</title>
  <script src="https://ajax.googleapis.com/ajax/libs/angularjs/1.6.4/angular.min.js"></script>
 </head>
 <body>
  <h1>Variable Addition Operation</h1>
   <div ng-app="" ng-init="labor=20;materials=10">
   Total Prime Costs
   {{labor+materials}}
   </div>
 </body>
</html>
```

Notice that the ng-init directive was used to assign the variables labor and materials to the numbers 20 and 10, respectively within the view. If you've been using other programming languages, you'll recognize that this is the typical way to define local variables. The code uses the two local variables to get the total values of the numbers stored within the variables.

You'll likely see the following result once you run the code in the browser:

ANGULARJS EXPRESSIONS WITH STRINGS

Expressions can work just as well with strings. The following code defines two strings named "firstName" and "lastName" and uses expressions to display their value:

```
<!doctype html>
<html ng-app>
  <head>
    <title>AngularJS Expressions</title>
    <script src="https://ajax.googleapis.com/ajax/libs/angularjs/1.6.4/angular.min.js"></script>
  </head>
  <body>
  <h1>Expressions with Strings</h1>
    <div ng-app="" ng-init="firstName='Jack';lastName='Jameson'">
    First Name: {{firstName}} <br>
    Last Name: {{lastName}}
    </div>
  </body>
</html>
```

Notice that the ng-init directive was used to assign the variables firstName and lastName to the values 'Jack' and 'Jameson', respectively. The expressions {{firstName}} and {{lastName}} are then used to access each variable's value and show them in the view.

When you execute the code, you will see the following result:

ANGULARJS EXPRESSIONS WITH ARRAYS

AngularJS likewise works well with arrays. This code defines an array which holds the marks of a student in five subjects and displays the values in the view:

```
<!doctype html>
<html ng-app>
  <head>
    <title>AngularJS Expressions</title>
    <script src="https://ajax.googleapis.com/ajax/libs/angularjs/1.6.4/angular.min.js"></script>
  </head>
  <body>
    <h1>Expressions with Arrays</h1>
      <div ng-app="" ng-init="marks=[90,86,79,88,92]">
        Student Grades <br>
        Subject1: {{marks[0]}} <br>
        Subject2: {{marks[1]}} <br>
        Subject3: {{marks[2]}} <br>
        Subject4: {{marks[3]}} <br>
        Subject5: {{marks[4]}} <br>
      </div>
  </body>
</html>
```

The ng-init directive was used to define an array called "marks" having the values of 90, 86, 79, 88, and 92. The expressions of marks with a specified index are then used to access each object in the array. Notice that indexing starts at zero. Hence, Subject1 takes the zero index in the 'marks' array.

When you execute the code in the browser, here's what the output might be:

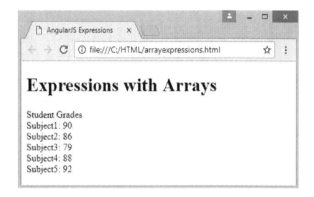

ANGULARJS EXPRESSIONS WITH JAVASCRIPT OBJECTS

AngularJS expressions can likewise be used with JavaScript objects which are name-value pairs.

Here is an example of a statement that creates a JavaScript object:

var items = {animal:"dog", color:"blue", ocean:"Pacific Ocean"};

The following code will define an object named 'student' with three key value pairs:

```
<!doctype html>
<html ng-app>
 <head>
  <title>AngularJS Expressions</title>
  <script src="https://ajax.googleapis.com/ajax/libs/angularjs/1.6.4/angular.min.js"></script>
 </head>
 <body>
  <h1>Expressions with Arrays</h1>
   <div ng-app="" ng-init="student={firstName:'Jacques',lastName:'Amber', age:18}">
    Student Data <br>
    First Name: {{student.firstName}} <br>
    Last Name: {{student.lastName}} <br>
    Age: {{student.age}}
   </div>
 </body>
</html>
```

The code uses the ng-init directive to define an object named student. The object student has three key-value pairs, namely, firstName with the value of Jacques, lastName with the value of Amber, and age with a value of 18.

The expressions {{student.firstName}}, {{student.lastName}}, and {{student.age}} were used to access the value for each key and output them in the view. Notice that the dot (.) notation was used to access the values.

When you execute the code on the browser, here's what it might display:

Summary:

AngularJS expressions can be used to evaluate expressions like addition or multiplication of numbers.

The ng-init directive is used to define variables that can be displayed in the view.

Expressions can work with primitive data types like numbers and strings and with arrays and Javascript objects.

AngularJS expressions are as powerful and flexible as JavaScript expressions. However, it has its limitations such as inability to use functions and regular expressions and the absence of support for conditional statements or loops.

CHAPTER 8: FILTERS

Filters are used to format data or values of an expression. AngularJS filters allow you to display pieces of data to the users the way you want them to view the data. For instance, you can use filters to display the string in either uppercase or lowercase. Similarly, you can use filters to display numbers in the desired format. In this chapter, you will learn how the different filters in AngularJS are used and how you can make custom filters for your application.

BUILT-IN FILTERS

AngularJS provides the following built-in filters:

lowercase	formats a string/text to lower case
uppercase	formats a string/text to upper case
number	controls the appearance of the number and limits the number of decimal points that will be displayed
currency	formats a number to a currency format.
orderby	orders the array based on a given expression
filter	filters a subset of items from arrays
date	formats a date to a given format.
limitTo	limits a string/array to a given number of characters/elements
json	formats an object to a JSON string

Lowercase

The lowercase filter takes and formats a string output and displays all characters as lowercase.

In the following example, the Controller will send a string to the View through the scope object. Instead of changing the string in the controller, you can use the lowercase filter in the View to display the string in lowercase.

```
<!DOCTYPE html>
<html>
<script src="https://ajax.googleapis.com/ajax/libs/angularjs/1.6.4/angular.min.js"></script>
<body>

<div ng-app="myApp" ng-controller="studentCtrl">

<p>His last name is {{ lastName | lowercase }}.</p>

</div>

<script>
angular.module('myApp', []).controller('studentCtrl', function($scope) {
    $scope.firstName = "Leonard",
    $scope.lastName = "Brown"
});
</script>

</body>
</html>
```

The above code passes two strings, "Leonard" and "Brown", which are combinations of uppercase and lowercase characters in member variables firstName and lastName and attaches them to the scope object. The filter (|) symbol is used for the member variable lastName to indicate that the output should be formatted with a filter. The lowercase keyword is then used to output the specified string in lowercase.

When you run the code, here's what the result should be:

Uppercase

The uppercase filter takes and formats a string output and displays all characters as uppercase.

In the following example, the Controller will send a string to the View through the scope object. It uses the uppercase filter in the View to display the string in uppercase.

```
<!DOCTYPE html>
<html>
<script src="https://ajax.googleapis.com/ajax/libs/angularjs/1.6.4/angular.min.js"></script>
<body>

<div ng-app="myApp" ng-controller="studentCtrl">

<p>His last name is {{ lastName | uppercase }}.</p>

</div>

<script>
angular.module('myApp', []).controller('studentCtrl', function($scope) {
    $scope.firstName = "Leonard",
    $scope.lastName = "Brown"
});
</script>

</body>
</html>
```

The above example uses the keyword 'uppercase' to format and display the output string 'lastName' in uppercase letters.

When you run the code, here's what the output might be like:

Number

The number filter is used to format a number and impose a limit on the number of decimal points that should be displayed for the number.

The following example will show how the number filter is used to restrict the display of a number to two decimal places. It will use a controller to send a given number to the View through a scope object. The filter or pipe (|) symbol will then be used in the View along with the keyword number to format the specified number.

```
<!DOCTYPE html>
<html>
<script src="https://ajax.googleapis.com/ajax/libs/angularjs/1.6.4/angular.min.js"></script>
<body>

<div ng-app="myApp" ng-controller="bookCtrl">

<p>The reference number is {{ reference | number:2 }}.</p>

</div>

<script>
angular.module('myApp', []).controller('bookCtrl', function($scope) {
    $scope.reference = 38.96754213;
});
</script>

</body>
</html>
```

The above code passes the number 38.96754213 in the member variable reference and attaches them to the scope object. The pipe (|) symbol is then used for the variable reference to indicate that the output should be formatted with a filter. The number keyword and the number '2' is used to output the given number to a number with two decimal places.

When you run the code, here's what the output might be:

Take note that the number filter did not simply drop the rest of the decimal places but rounded the number off to the nearest hundredths.

Currency

The currency filter is used to apply the currency format to a number. For instance, if you want to display a number with a currency prefix like $, you can use this filter.

The following example uses a controller to output a number to the View through a scope object. The currency filter is then used to format the output.

```
<!DOCTYPE html>
<html>
<script src="https://ajax.googleapis.com/ajax/libs/angularjs/1.6.4/angular.min.js"></script>
<body>

<div ng-app="myApp" ng-controller="chargesCtrl">

<p>The total bill is {{ fees | currency }}.</p>

</div>

<script>
angular.module('myApp', []).controller('chargesCtrl', function($scope) {
    $scope.fees = 34679.8897;
});
</script>

</body>
</html>
```

The above code passes a number with four decimal places to the member variable 'fees' and attaches it to the scope object. The pipe (|) symbol is then used with the currency filter to format the output. Take note that this filter will apply the currency symbol specified in your computer's language setting.

If you run the code, here's what the result might be like:

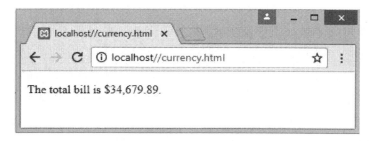

Notice that the currency filter rounded off the number to two decimal points instead of merely dropping the rest of the decimal points.

Filter

The filter 'filter' is used to select a subset of an array. This filter returns an array with objects that match the given criteria.

The following code uses the ng-repeat directive to evaluate the array passed to the scope object names of the namesController. It uses the pipe (|) symbol to indicate the use of a filter. It then applies the keyword filter with letter "e" as the criteria for the output.

```
<!DOCTYPE html>
<html>
<script src="https://ajax.googleapis.com/ajax/libs/angularjs/1.6.4/angular.min.js"></script>
<body>

<div ng-app="myApp" ng-controller="namesController">

<ul>
 <li ng-repeat="x in names | filter : 'e'">
  {{ x }}
 </li>
</ul>

</div>

<script>
angular.module('myApp', []).controller('namesController', function($scope) {
    $scope.names = [
        'Jane',
        'Mike',
        'Dorothy',
        'Kim',
        'Joseph',
        'Arthur',
        'Halden',
        'James',
        'Kaye'
    ];
});
</script>

<p>This code displays names containing the letter "e".</p>

</body>
</html>
```

When you run the code, the output would be:

71

Filtering an Array Based on the User's Input

You can also use an input field's value as the expression in a filter by setting the ng-model directive on it.

In the following example, the list of names will either shrink or grow depending on how many names will match the letter that will be typed in the input field.

```
<!DOCTYPE html>
<html>
<script src="https://ajax.googleapis.com/ajax/libs/angularjs/1.6.4/angular.min.js"></script>
<body>
<div ng-app="myApp" ng-controller="namesController">
<p>Type a letter in the box:</p>
<p><input type="text" ng-model="test"></p>
<ul>
  <li ng-repeat="x in names | filter:test">
    {{ x }}
  </li>
</ul>
</div>

<script>
angular.module('myApp', []).controller('namesController', function($scope) {
    $scope.names = [
        'Jane',
        'Mike',
        'Dorothy',
        'Kim',
        'Joseph',
        'Arthur',
        'Halden',
        'James',
        'Kaye'
    ];
});
</script>
<p>This list only includes names that match the specified filter.</p>
</body>
</html>
```

When you run the code and type the letter 'h' on the input box, here's what the output will be:

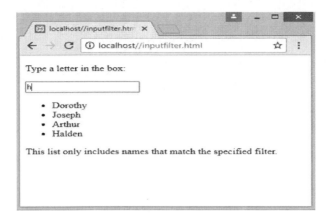

CUSTOM FILTERS

In some cases, the standard filters in AngularJS may not be sufficient to satisfy the requirements for formatting output. AngularJS lets you create custom filter which will pass the required output.

The following code will use a Controller to pass a string to the View. However, the string should not be displayed as is and requires some formatting. To make sure that the string will always be displayed in a particular format, a custom filter will be used to append another string. The combined string will then be displayed to the user.

```
<html>
<script src="https://ajax.googleapis.com/ajax/libs/angularjs/1.6.4/angular.min.js"></script>
<body>
<h1>World Events</h1>
<div ng-app="myApp" ng-controller="sampleCtrl">

  The event is {{event|Customfilter}}

<script>
var app = angular.module('myApp', []);

app.filter('Customfilter', function() {

  return function(input)
  {
    return input + " Event";
  }
  });

app.controller('sampleCtrl', function($scope) {
  $scope.event = "Global Trade Exhibit";
  });
</script>
</body>
</html>
```

The above example passes the string "Global Trade Exhibit" in a member variable named 'event' and attaches the string to the $scope object.

Angular's filter service is used to create a custom filter. In the above example, the custom filter was defined and given the name 'Customfilter'. The filter definition also specified a function that will return a function. This function contains the code that will be used to create a custom filter. In this example, the string "Event" will be appended to the string "Global Trade Exhibit" which was passed from the view to the filter.

The code uses the Customfilter on the member variable 'event'.

When you execute the code, here's what the result will be:

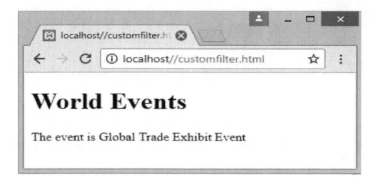

Summary:

Filters allow you to control how the output will be displayed to users.

AngularJS provides several standard filters such as uppercase and lowercase filter to change strings output to uppercase and lowercase respectively.

The number filter lets you specify the number of decimal points that will be displayed and, consequently, change the way numbers will be displayed.

The currency filter is used to add the default currency symbol to a number.

AngularJS likewise allows you to filter JSON-like strings to JSON specific format using the JSON filter.

If all other standard filters fail to provide the output that you need, you can create a custom filter using your own code to achieve the desired result.

CHAPTER 9: SCOPE

Scope is a JavaScript object that binds the Controller with the View (HTML). It contains the model data and has methods and properties that can be accessed by both the View and the Controller. In a controller, the model data can be accessed through the $scope object. To use the scope, you need to pass the $scope object as an argument in the controller.

To demonstrate, here's a code snippet that defines a function in the colorController and passes the $scope object as an argument:

```
<script>
  var mainApp = angular.module("mainApp", []);

  mainApp.controller("colorController", function($scope) {
    $scope.caption = "In color controller";
    $scope.label = "Color";
  });
</script>
```

Here are the important points in the example:

The $scope object was passed as an argument to the colorController at the same time that the controller was defined.

The $scope.caption and $scope.label are the models that will be used in the HTML page.

The values for the said models are provided in the application module under the colorController.

Scope Inheritance

Scopes are controller-specific. When you define nested controllers, the child controller will inherit the $scope of the main controller.

The following is a code that uses a nested controller:

```
<script>
  var myApp = angular.module("myApp", []);
  myApp.controller("colorController", function($scope) {
    $scope.greeting = "It's a colorful world!";
    $scope.type = "color";
  });
  myApp.controller("primaryController", function($scope) {
    $scope.greeting = "The colors of the rainbow";
  });
</script>
```

Here are the key points in the above example:

Values were assigned to models in 'colorController.

The 'greeting' in the shapeController was overridden in the primaryController, the child controller. Hence, whenever the 'greeting' variable is used within the primaryController, the 'greeting' value will override the value defined in the colorController, the parent controller.

CHAPTER 10: MODULES

In AngularsJS, modules are containers of the various parts of an application. They are used to separate filters, controllers, service, etc. and help keep the code clean.

AngularJS modules have two important roles to play:

- Define the application functionality that will be applied globally with the use of the ng-app directive
- Define functionalities such as filters, directives and services to make it easy to reuse them in different applications

Modules and Controllers

Current trends in web applications development using AngularJS favor the practice of creating multiple controllers and modules. This principle supports a logical separation of multiple levels of functionalities.

In general, modules are stored in JavaScript files outside of the main application file.

The following example will demonstrate how the external modules interact with application files:

First, you will have to create a file called Operations which will contain two modules. One module will perform the functionality of multiplication while the other module will perform the functionality of division.

Next, you will create two application files that will access the

Operations file. The first application file will access the multiplication module while the second application will access the division module.

Step 1: Create the code for the modules and controllers of the Operations file:

```
var MultiplicationApp = angular.module('MultiplicationApp',[]);
MultiplicationApp.controller('MultiplicationController', function($scope) {
    $scope.a=10;
    $scope.b=2;
    $scope.c=$scope.a * $scope.b;
});
var DivisionApp = angular.module('DivisionApp',[]);
DivisionApp.controller('DivisionAppController', function($scope) {
    $scope.a=12;
    $scope.b=3;
    $scope.d=$scope.a / $scope.b;
});
```

Take note of the following points from the above code:

The code created two Angular modules. One is called 'MultiplicationApp' and the other is called 'DivisionApp':

```
var              MultiplicationApp              =
angular.module('MultiplicationApp',[]);
```

```
var DivisionApp = angular.module('DivisionApp',[]);
```

The code created two controllers for each module. One is named 'MultiplicationController' while the other is named 'DivisionController'. These controllers hold different logic for multiplication and division of numbers.

```
MultiplicationApp.controller('MultiplicationController', function($scope) {
```

```
DivisionApp.controller('DivisionAppController', function($scope) {
```

Step 2: Create the main application files. You can name the

first file as 'ApplicationMultiplication.html. Use the following code:

```
<!DOCTYPE html>
<html>
<head>
  <meta charset="UTF-8">
  <title>Multiplication</title>
    <script src="http://ajax.googleapis.com/ajax/libs/angularjs/1.6.4/angular.min.js"></script>
    <script src=cdn.mysite.com"Operations.js"></script>
</head>
<body>
<div ng-app = "MultiplicationApp" ng-controller="MultiplicationController">
  {{c}}
</div>
</script>
</body>
</html>
```

Take note of the following points in the code:

<script src=cdn.mysite.com"Operations.js"></script>

This line references the Operations.js file. This will allow the main application to access the AngularJS modules stored in the file.

<div ng-app = "MultiplicationApp" ng-controller="MultiplicationController">

The above line of code uses the ng-app and the ng-controller directives to access the MultiplicationApp module.

{{c}}

Referencing the Multiplication module and controller in the main application file will allow you to access the $scope.c variable using an expression. The expression {{c}} is the product of the multiplication operation performed on the two scope variables named 'a' and 'b' using the MultiplicationController.

You will take the same steps to make use of the DivisionApp:

Step 3: Create the main application file. You will name this file as 'ApplicationDivision.html. You can use the following code:

```
<!DOCTYPE html>
<html>
<head>
  <meta charset="UTF-8">
  <title>Division</title>
    <script src="http://ajax.googleapis.com/ajax/libs/angularjs/1.6.4/angular.min.js"></script>
<script src="//cdn.mysite.com/lib/Operations.js"></script>
</head>
<body>
<div ng-app = "DivisionApp" ng-controller="DivisionController">
  {{d}}
</div>
</script>
</body>
</html>
```

Take note of the following important points:

<script src="//cdn.mysite.com/lib/Operations.js"></script>

This line in the code references the Operations.js file. This allows the main application to access the AngularJS modules stored in the file.

<div ng-app = "DivisionApp" ng-controller="DivisionController">

This line of code uses the ng-app and the ng-controller directives to access the DivisionApp module.

{{d}}

Referencing the Division module and controller in the main application file will allow you to access the $scope.d variable using an expression. The expression {{d}} is the result of the division operation performed on the two scope variables named 'a' and 'b' through the controller DivisionController.

Summary:

The use of modules prevents application controllers from assuming a global scope.

You can create multiple modules to separate business logic as well as logic within the different modules.

You can define and assign a set of controllers to each Angular JS module.

AngularJS controllers and modules are typically defined in different Javascript files. You can reference these files in your main application file.

CHAPTER 11: EVENTS

Web applications typically need to deal with DOM events such as keyboard presses, mouse click, and moves. You can add AngularJS functionality to manage these events. For instance, you can use the ng-click event directive to perform a process when the user clicks on a button.

In this chapter, you learn the different Event directives in AngularJS.

THE NG-CLICK DIRECTIVE

The ng-click directive can be used to add custom behavior whenever an HTML element is clicked. You will generally use this for a button as this is where you will usually add events that respond to the user's mouse clicks.

The following example shows how the click event is implemented:

```
<!DOCTYPE html>
<html>
<script
src="https://ajax.googleapis.com/ajax/libs/angularjs/1.6.4/angular.min.js">
</script>
<body>

<div ng-app="myApp" ng-controller="myCtrl">

<button ng-click="count = count + 1" ng-init="count=0">
    Click Me!</button>

<p>The current count is {{ count }}</p>

</div>
<script>
var app = angular.module('myApp', []);
app.controller('myCtrl', function($scope) {
    $scope.count = 0;
});
</script>

</body>
</html>
```

The code contains a counter variable that increments in value whenever the button is clicked.

The code uses the ng-init directive to initialize the value of the local variable by setting it to zero (0).

It applies the ng-click directive to a button. Specifically, the code within the directive will increment the counter variable by one.

In the view, the script will display the current value of the counter variable to users.

When executed, the following output will be displayed in your browser:

Click Me!

The current count is 0

It shows that the current count is zero. If you click on the button, the value will increment by one:

Click Me!

The current count is 1

USING NG-SHOW TO DISPLAY HTML ELEMENTS

You can hide or display a specified HTML element using the ng-show directive. This is done in the background by adding or removing the ng-hide CSS class to the element.

In the following example, the ng-show event directive was used to show a hidden element:

```
<!DOCTYPE html>
<html>
<script
src="https://ajax.googleapis.com/ajax/libs/angularjs/1.6.4/angular.min.js">
</script>
<body>

<div ng-app="myApp" ng-controller="eventCtrl">

<input type="button" value="Show this Month's Event" ng-click="ShowHide()"/>
<br><br><div ng-show = "IsVisible">Global Trade Show</div>
<script>
var app = angular.module('myApp', []);
app.controller('eventCtrl', function($scope) {
    $scope.IsVisible = false;
    $scope.ShowHide = function() {
       $scope.IsVisible = $scope.IsVisible = true;
    }
    });
</script>

</body>
</html>
```

Key Points of the Code:

The ng-click directive was attached to the button element. This script references a function named "ShowHide" which was defined in the controller eventCtrl.

The ng-show attribute was attached to a <div> that holds the text "Global Trade Show". This tag will either be hidden or displayed depending on the ng-show attribute.

The "IsVisible" member variable was attached to the $scope object within the EventController. Its attribute will then be passed to the ng-show attribute to handle the div control's visibility. In this code, this was initially set to 'false' which means that the <div> tag will be hidden when the page is displayed for the first time.

Conversely, when the ng-show attribute is set to true, the <div> tag will be displayed to the user.

A code was added to the ShowHide function which sets the IsVisible variable to true. This means that the application will show the <div> data to the user.

Here's the output:

Show this Month's Event

Initially, the <div> data that contains the text "Global Trade Show" was not displayed. Remember that the initial value of the isVisible $scope object was set to false. This was the value that was passed to the <div> tag's ng-show directive.

If you click on the "Show Event" button, this causes the isVisible variable to change to 'true' which, in turn, triggers the display of the text "Global Trade Show". Here's the result:

Show this Month's Event

Global Trade Show

USING NG-HIDE TO HIDE HTML ELEMENTS

The ng-hide directive works like the ng-show directive but does the reverse: it hides the element if the expression is true and shows the element if the expression is false.

The following example retains the settings used to demonstrate the ng-show directive in the earlier example. This time, though, it uses the ng-hide directive.

```
<!DOCTYPE html>
<html>
<script
src="https://ajax.googleapis.com/ajax/libs/angularjs/1.6.4/angular.min.js">
</script>
<body>

<div ng-app="myApp" ng-controller="eventCtrl">

<input type="button" value="Show this Month's Event" ng-click="ShowHide()"/>
<br><br><div ng-hide = "IsVisible">Global Trade Show</div>
<script>
var app = angular.module('myApp', []);
app.controller('eventCtrl', function($scope) {
    $scope.IsVisible = false;
    $scope.ShowHide = function() {
        $scope.IsVisible = $scope.IsVisible = true;
    }
});
</script>

</body>
</html>
```

The ng-click directive was attached to the button element. This script references a function named "ShowHide" which was defined in the controller eventController.

The ng-hide attribute was attached to a <div> that holds the text "Global Trade Show". This tag will either be hidden or displayed depending on the isVisible attribute.

The "IsVisible" member variable was attached to the $scope object within the eventController. Its attribute will then be passed to the ng-hide attribute to handle the <div> control's visibility.

In this code, this was initially set to 'false' which means that the web page will initially display the <div> content. Conversely, when the ng-show attribute is set to true, the <div> tag will be hidden by default. A code was also added to the ShowHide function which sets the IsVisible variable to true. This will allow the application to hide the <div> content to the user.

If you run the code, the web browser will display the following:

```
[ Show this Month's Event ]
```

Global Trade Show

Summary:

AngularJS provides the Events directives ng-click, ng-show, and ng-hide to add custom code that can be used to respond to user- generated events like keyboard entries and clicks.

The ng-click is the most commonly used Events directive. It is used to create codes that will direct the application to perform tasks in response to button clicks.

HTML elements can be shown or hidden to users using the ng-hide or ng-show attributes.

CHAPTER 12: SELECT BOXES

AngularJS allows you to create a dropdown list based on an object or elements of an array.

The ng-repeat directive can be used to repeat the execution of a block of code for each array element. This makes it capable of creating options that can be used in dropdown lists. The ng-repeat directive, however, is currently limited to handling string values.

The AngularJS documentation recommends the use of the ng-options directive for creating dropdown lists. This directive is specifically provided for generating a dropdown list with options. It is used to create a list of items within the <select> element.

While you can use the ng-repeat directive in place of ng-options to achieve the same result in many cases, the use of ng-options offers some advantages:

It allows greater flexibility in terms of determining how the select's model should be assigned within the comprehension expression.

Because it does not create the options individually, the use of ng-options greatly improves rendering speed.

It helps reduce memory usage because you need not create a new scope with every repeated instance.

Another distinct benefit of using ng-options over the ng-repeat directive is its capability to handle non-string objects for selected values. This allows the value to store more types of information which can make your application more flexible.

To demonstrate how the ng-repeat and ng-options directive work on arrays, you can use the following array data:

```
$scope.subjects = [
    {subject : "Mathematics", session : "PM"},
    {subject : "Science", session : "AM"},
    {subject : "Geography", session : "AM"}
];
```

The following example uses the ng-repeat directive. With this directive, you can only select and display a single value.

```
<div ng-app="myApp" ng-controller="myCtrl">

<p>Select a subject:</p>

<select ng-model="selectedsubject">
<option ng-repeat="x in subjects" value="{{x.subject}}">{{x.subject}}</option>
</select>

<h1>You have chosen: {{selectedsubject}}</h1>

</div>

<script>
var app = angular.module('myApp', []);
app.controller('myCtrl', function($scope) {
    $scope.subjects = [
        {subject : "Mathematics", session : "PM"},
        {subject : "Science", session : "AM"},
        {subject : "Geography", session : "AM"}
    ];
});
</script>

</body>
</html>
```

When you run the above code and click on the select option, here's what the dropdown list may show:

On the other hand, the following code uses the ng-options directive to create a dropdown list based on the same array data:

```
<!DOCTYPE html>
<html>
<script src="https://ajax.googleapis.com/ajax/libs/angularjs/1.6.4/angular.min.js"></script>
<body>

<div ng-app="myApp" ng-controller="myCtrl">

<p>Select a subject:</p>

<select ng-model="selectedSubjects" ng-options="x.subject for x in subjects">
</select>

<h1>You have chosen: {{selectedSubjects.subject}}</h1>
<h2>Its schedule is: {{selectedSubjects.session}}</h2>


</div>

<script>
var app = angular.module('myApp', []);
app.controller('myCtrl', function($scope) {
    $scope.subjects = [
        {subject : "Mathematics", session : "PM"},
        {subject : "Science", session : "AM"},
        {subject : "Geography", session : "AM"}
    ];
});
</script>

</body>
</html>
```

When you run the code, here's how the web page would look if you choose the subject Mathematics from the dropdown list:

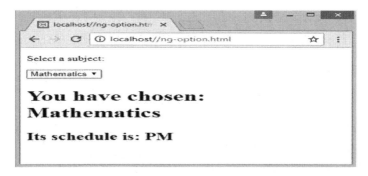

By using ng-options, the code was able to display both the subject and the session.

Using the Data Source as Object

You have seen how an array was used as a source of data for your dropdown list. With ng-options, you can also use objects as options in the select list.

To demonstrate, here's an object containing three key-value pairs:

```
$scope.subjects = {
    subject101 : "Mathematics",
    subject102 : "Science",
    subject103 : "Geography"
};
```

The following code uses an object as a source of data. Take note of the slight difference in the expression for the ng-options property:

```
<select ng-model="selectedSubject" ng-options="x for (x, y) in subjects">
```

It names the object 'subjects' as the source of data and specifies 'x' as the option in the select box. In this statement, x stands for the 'key' and 'y' stands for the value of the key.

```
<!DOCTYPE html>
<html>
<script src="https://ajax.googleapis.com/ajax/libs/angularjs/1.6.4/angular.min.js"></script>
<body>

<div ng-app="myApp" ng-controller="myCtrl">

<p>Choose a subject:</p>

<select ng-model="selectedSubject" ng-options="x for (x, y) in subjects">
</select>

<h1>You have chosen: {{selectedSubject}}</h1>

</div>

<p>This codes uses an object as the data source in a dropdown list.</p>

<script>
var app = angular.module('myApp', []);
app.controller('myCtrl', function($scope) {
    $scope.subjects = {
        subject101 : "Mathematics",
        subject102 : "Science",
        subject103 : "Geography"
    }
});
</script>

</body>
</html>
```

If you run the code, the 'keys' in the specified key-value pairs will be displayed as options in the dropdown list:

93

Assuming you have chosen subject102, here's what the web page will display:

CHAPTER 13: SERVICES

Services are Javascript functions that are responsible for specific tasks and are limited to a particular AngularJS application. A service is an individual entity that can be tested and maintained and can be called by controllers when needed. It is only instantiated whenever required by a component of an application. Services provide a way to organize your code and share it across the application.

AngularJS provides a wide range of built-in services that include $location, $window, $https:, and $route. Each of these services performs a particular task and are always written with a $ prefix.

The $http Service

The $http service is used to make a request to the server. It returns the response and allows an application to handle the response.

The following example uses this built-in service to request data from the server and assigns the response as the value of myGreetings variable:

```
<div ng-app="newApp" ng-controller="newCtrl">

<p>Today's greeting is:</p>
<h1>{{myGreeting}}</h1>

</div>
<script>
var myapp = angular.module('newApp', []);
```

```
app.controller(newCtrl', function($scope, $http) {
  $http.get("greeting.htm")
  .then(function(response) {
    $scope.myGreeting = response.data;
  });
});
</script>
```

The above code accesses the web page "greeting.htm" and returns the response in a header. It uses the .get method ($http.get), one of the shortcut methods of the $http service. The other shortcut methods are as follows:

.post()
.head()
.delete()
.patch()
.jsonp()
.put()

The server's response is an object that possesses the following attributes:

.data	It is an object or string that carries the server's response.
.config	This is the object that will be used to produce a request.
.statusText	This is a string that defines the HTTP status.
.status	It is a number that defines the HTTP status.
.headers	This is a function that will be used to fetch header data.

This example will demonstrate the various shortcut methods of the $http service:

```
var myapp = angular.module('newApp', []);
app.controller('newCtrl', function($scope, $http) {
    $http.get("greeting.htm")
    .then(function(response) {
        $scope.content = response.data;
        $scope.statuscode = response.status;
        $scope.statustext = response.statustext;
    });
});
```

CHAPTER 14: THE NG-MODEL DIRECTIVE

The ng-model directive represents the models in AngularJS. Its main purpose is to attach the View to the Model. It ensures that the data entered in the View matches that which is stored in the Model. For instance, if you have a single page that collects users' input on textbox fields for names; you can map the same field to your data model using the ng-model directive. This directive will ensure that the model and data in the view are always synchronized.

Functions of the ng-model directive

You have learned that the main purpose of the ng-model is to bind the data in the model to that of the view displayed to users. Specifically, the ng-model performs the following:

It binds HTML controls such as select, text area, and input in View to the model.

It provides a validation behavior such as restrictions on the data type that can be entered on a textbox.

It maintains control over the synchronization state between the View and the data such that whenever data values change, it automatically changes the value in the model.

Applying ng-model to input element, text area, and select elements

Input elements

The ng-model attribute can be used on the input elements such as check boxes, text boxes, radio button, etc.

The following example will show a text input type with 2 checkboxes. One checkbox will be marked as default while the other will not be marked.

```
<html>
<script
src="https://ajax.googleapis.com/ajax/libs/angularjs/1.6.4/angular.min.js">
</script>
<body>

<div ng-app="myApp" ng-controller="themesCtrl">
<form>
Name: <input type="text" ng-model="uName"><br>
Theme: <br>

<input type="checkbox" ng-model="Themes.Standard">Standard<br>
<input type="checkbox" ng-model="Themes.Premium">Premium
</form></div>

<script>
var app = angular.module('myApp', []);
app.controller('themesCtrl', function($scope) {
    $scope.uName = "John Swish";
    $scope.Themes =
    {
    Standard : true,
    Premium : false
    };
    });
</script>
</body>
</html>
```

In the above code, the ng-model directive was used to bind "uName", a member variable, to the input type text control. The uName variable will later hold the string 'John Swish'. You can assign any name to the member variable.

The code defines the first checkbox, "Standard", and binds it to the member variable 'Themes.Standard'.

The code also defines another checkbox named "Premium" and binds it to the member variable 'Themes.Premium.

Likewise, the member variable named "uName" was attached and assigned the value of 'John Swish'.

A member array variable named "Themes" was declared and given two values – "true" and "false". The checkbox with the value of "true" will be marked with a check while the checkbox with the value of "false" will not be marked.

If you run the code, this will be the output:

Name: John Swish
Theme:
☑ Standard
☐ Premium

Notice that the checkbox for Standard was marked by default.

Applying ng-model to select element

You can also apply the ng-model directive to the select tag and use it to populate the select list.

The following example will show a text input type with the value of "John Swish" and a select list containing 2 items called "Standard" and "Premium".

```html
<html>
<script
src="https://ajax.googleapis.com/ajax/libs/angularjs/1.6.4/angular.min.js">
</script>
<body>

<div ng-app="myApp" ng-controller="themesCtrl">
<form>
Name: <input type="text" ng-model="uName" value="John Swish"><br>
Theme: <br>
<select ng-model="Themes">
<option>{{Themes.option1}}</option>
<option>{{Themes.option2}}</option>
</select>
</form></div>
<script>
var app = angular.module('myApp', []);
app.controller('themesCtrl', function($scope) {
    $scope.uName = "John Swish";
    $scope.Themes =
    {
    option1 : "Standard",
    option2 : "Premium"
    };
    });
</script>
</body>
</html>
```

The code uses the ng-model directive to bind "Themes", a member variable, to the select type control. Within the select control, the member variables Themes.option1 and Themes.option2 were attached to the first option and second option, respectively.

The Themes array variable was assigned to two key-value pairs. The first takes the value of "Standard" while the second hold the value of "Premium". Both were passed to the select input tag and displayed.

If you run the code, the web browser will display the following:

Name: John Swish

Theme:

If you click on the select box, you will see two options:

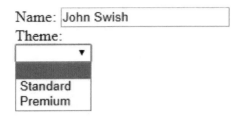

Applying ng-model to textarea

The textarea tag is used to specify an input area containing unlimited number of text/characters. The text is rendered in a fixed-width or monospace font. Text areas are commonly used inside a parent<form> element.

The following example will demonstrate how you can pass several lines of string from a Controller to a View and bind the value to the textarea control.

```
<!DOCTYPE html>
<html>
<script src="https://ajax.googleapis.com/ajax/libs/angularjs/1.6.4/angular.min.js"></script>
<body>
<h1>A Worldwide Event</h1>
<div ng-app="MyApp" ng-controller="TopCtrl">
<form>
   Event Description: <br><br>
   
<textarea rows="5" cols="50" ng-model="eDescription"></textarea><br>
</form>
</div>
<script>
var app=angular.module('MyApp', []);
app.controller('TopCtrl', function($scope){
$scope.eDescription="This is a worldwide cultural event \nA quadrennial feast"
});
</script>
</body>
</html>
```

The code used the ng-model directive to bind "eDescription, a member variable, to "textarea" control. This variable will eventually hold the text/characters that will be passed to the textarea. Inside the textarea tag, the value of 4 was specified for the row while the value of 50 was defined for the columns. These attributes set the space required to display several lines of text.

The member variable "eDescription" was bound to the scope object named eDescription ($scope.eDescription) as a string value was passed to the variable.

Notice the /n literal which was used to split the string into several lines. This new line character sets up the string to be displayed into several lines in the textarea control.

When you run the code, here's what the output might be:

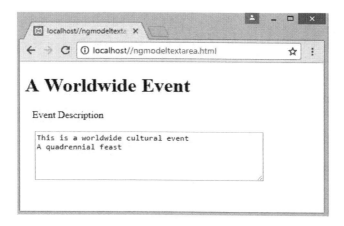

Summary

In AngularJS, the ng-model directive is used to represent the model. Its main objective is to attach the view to the model. This directive can be attached to checkbox and text controls to make them more interactive during runtime. Likewise, it can be attached to a textarea control and allow multiple lines of strings to be displayed to the View through the Controller. Finally, the ng-model directive is used to fill a list of options that will be shown to the user.

CHAPTER 15: ROUTING

A Single Page Application (SPA) is a web application that loads a single web page and dynamically updates the page based on user interaction.

Almost all modern web page applications implement the SPA concept. AngularJS implements SPAs through routing. Routes let you set up a unique URL for the different content in a web application and allow you to show multiple content based on the user's action.

To demonstrate how routes work, you can take a website hosted through the URL http://mysite.com/index as an example. This URL hosts the main page of the application. Assuming that the application will handle a series of events and will give users the option to view the list of these events, learn more about a specific event, or remove an event, enabling routing would make these functionalities available in a single page application. In this scenario, such options would be handled with these links:

http://mysite.com/index.html#ListEvents

http://mysite.com/index.html#DisplayEvent

http://mysite.com/index.html#DeleteEvent

Take note that the routes (ListEvents, DisplayEvent, and DeleteEvent) were placed after the hashtag (#) symbol. Meantime, the main URL remained the same.

ADDING ROUTES

AngularJS routes are used to direct the user to a different view without leaving the main HTML page.

To use routing in your application, you will have to perform these main steps:

Create a reference to angular-route.js. This file contains all the functionalities of routing. You have to place this JavaScript file in your application in order to access the modules that will be required to perform routing.

```
<script
src="https://ajax.googleapis.com/ajax/libs/angularjs/1.6.4/angular-route.js"
</script>
```

Include a dependency to the ngRoute module inside the application. This is another vital step because your application will not be able to implement routing functionalities without it.

Here's the statement to add this dependency:

```
var module = angular.module("sampleApp", ['ngRoute']);
```

Notice that the statement is the usual way you would declare a module except that this time, the 'ngRoute' was added.

Configure the $routeProvider. This step will provide the different routes the application may need.

Here's the syntax:

```
when(path, route)
```

The above statement indicates that when a specific path is selected, the associated route will be used to show the view requested by the user.

Add reference links within the HTML page. These links correspond to the different routes within the application.

Here's the syntax:

```
<a href="#/route1">Route 1</a><br/>
```

Use the ng-view directive. You will normally place this directive within a div tag. Its purpose is to inject the view's content whenever a particular route is selected.

The following example will demonstrate the above steps.

This application will present two links to the user. One link will display a list of local events while the other will show a list of global events. Whenever a user clicks on either link, the events for each category will be shown.

Step 1: Add angular-route.js as a script reference. You will need this file to access the functionalities of multiple routes/views. You can download the file from the AngularJS site.

```
<script
src="https://ajax.googleapis.com/ajax/libs/angularjs/1.6.4/angular-route.js"
</script>
```

Step 2: Add href tags to represent links to "Local Events" and "Global Events".

```
<a href="#!Local">Local Events</a>
<a href="#!Global">Global Events</a>
```

Step 3: Write an ng-view directive within the <div> tag to represent the view.

```
<div ng-view=""></div>
```

The above statement allows the associated view to be displayed when a user selects either option.

Step 4: Within the script tag for AngularS, include the '$routeProvider' service as well as the 'ngRoute module'.

```
var app = angular.module("myApp", ["ngRoute"]);
app.config(function($routeProvider) {
    $routeProvider
```

On the same block of code, you will create a route for both the #Local and #Global link:

```
var app = angular.module("myApp", ["ngRoute"]);
app.config(function($routeProvider) {
    $routeProvider
    .when("/Local", {
        templateUrl : "Local.html",
        controller : "localController"
    })
    .when("/Global", {
        templateUrl : "Global.html",
        controller : "globalController"
    });
});
```

The route for the Local link means that when the user clicks on the Local link, it will inject the Local.html file and call the localController to process the business logic.

The route of the Global link means that when the user clicks on the Global link, it will inject the Global.html file and call the globalController to process the business logic.

Step 5: Add two controllers that will handle the business logic for either options. You can name these controllers "localController" and "globalController".

For each controller, you will have to create an array consisting of several key-value pairs. These pairs will hold the Name and Description for each event. Likewise, add a variable to the scope object of both controllers. You can call this variable 'event'.

These blocks of code define the two controllers:

```
app.controller("localController", function ($scope) {
    $scope.event = [
    {Name: "Halloween Parade" Description="kiddie costume parade"}
    {Name: "Cookfest" Description="cooking contest"}
    {Name: "Dragon Boat Festival" Description="boat race"}
    ]

app.controller("globalController", function ($scope) {
    $scope.event = [
    {Name: "Festival International" Description="music festival}
    {Name: "Earth Day" Description="environmenal protection"}
    {Name: "Labor Day" Description="workers' day}
    ]
```

Here's how the entire code might look:

```
<!DOCTYPE html>
<html>
<script
src="https://ajax.googleapis.com/ajax/libs/angularjs/1.6.4/angular.min.js">
</script>
<script src="https://ajax.googleapis.com/ajax/libs/angularjs/1.6.4/angular-
route.js"></script>

<body ng-app="myApp">
<h1>Events Calendar</h1>
<li><a href="#!Local">Local Events</a></li>
<li><a href="#!Global">Global Events</a></li>
<div ng-view=""></div>
<script>
```

```
app.config(function($routeProvider) {
    $routeProvider
    .when("/Local", {
        templateUrl : "Local.html",
        controller : "localController"
    })
    .when("/Global", {
        templateUrl : "Global.html",
        controller : "globalController"
    });
});
app.controller("localController", function ($scope) {
    $scope.event = [
    {Name: "Halloween Parade", Description:"kiddie costume parade"},
    {Name: "Cookfest", Description:"cooking contest"},
    {Name: "Dragon Boat Festival", Description:"boat race"}
    ]
});
app.controller("globalController", function ($scope) {
    $scope.event = [
    {Name: "Festival International", Description:"music festival"},
    {Name: "Earth Day", Description:"environmental protection"},
    {Name: "Labor Day", Description:"workers' day"}
    ]
});
</script>
</body>
</html>
```

Step 6: Create two pages and name them Local.html and Global.html. Do the following steps for both pages to ensure that all key-value pairs will be shown on each page.

- Use the ng-repeat directive to access all key-value pairs.
- Display both name and description of all key-value pairs.

The files can be as simple as the following:

Local.html:

```
<h1>Local Events</h1>

<ul ng-repeat="item in event">
  <li> Event: {{item.Name}} - {{item.Description}}</li>

</ul>
```

Global.html:

<h1>Global Events</h1>

<ul ng-repeat="item in event">
  <li> Event: {{item.Name}} - {{item.Description}}</li>

</ul>

When you run the code, here's what the output might be:

Events Calendar

- Local Events
- Global Events

The browser displayed the reference links and the address bar indicated that the web page is Routing.html.

If you click on 'Local Events', here's what the browser will display:

Events Calendar

- Local Events
- Global Events

Local Events

- Event: Halloween Parade - kiddie costume parade

- Event: Cookfest - cooking contest

- Event: Dragon Boat Festival - boat race

The web browser displayed the array elements specified within the localController. Notice that the address bar indicates that you're still on the same page, Routing.html, but this time, this is followed by a hashtag # and the Local route.

If you click on 'Global Events', this will be the result:

Events Calendar

- Local Events
- Global Events

Global Events

- Event: Festival International - music festival

- Event: Earth Day - environmental protection

- Event: Labor Day - workers' day

The web browser displayed the array elements specified within the globalController. The address bar indicates that you're still on the Routing.html page but this time, it is followed by a hashtag # and the Global route.

ADDING A DEFAULT ROUTE

AngularJS routing likewise facilitates a default route. The HTML page redirects to this route if the current route has no match.

You can create a default route by adding this statement in the $routeProvider service definition statement:

```
.otherwise ({
   redirectTo: 'page'
});
```

The above statement causes the application to redirect to a specified page.

To demonstrate, assume that you want the web browser to display the Local route as the default view. Here's what the statement would be:

```
.otherwise({
   redirectTo:'/"Local"
});
```

The following snippet shows the inclusion of the 'otherwise' method within the route specification block:

```
var app = angular.module("myApp", ["ngRoute"]);
app.config(function($routeProvider) {
    $routeProvider
    .when("/Local", {
        templateUrl : "Local.html",
        controller : "localController"
    })
    .when("/Global", {
        templateUrl : "Global.html",
        controller : "globalController"
    })
    .otherwise({
        redirectTo:"/Local"
    });
});
```

If you run the code, the web browser will display this page:

Events Calendar

- Local Events
- Global Events

Local Events

- Event: Halloween Parade - kiddie costume parade

- Event: Cookfest - cooking contest

- Event: Dragon Boat Festival - boat race

The above result indicates that the routing service loads the Local route by default when the application starts and the viewer has not selected a link.

ACCESSING PARAMETERS FROM THE ROUTE

AngularJS likewise offers the functionality of providing parameters during routing. You can add the parameters just after the route.

This is the syntax for adding parameters:

HTMLPage#/route/parameter

For instance, assuming that the route's URL is http://mysite.com/index.html#/LocalEvents, you can add the parameter '1' at the end of the URL. The URL will then be: http://mysite.com/index.html#/LocalEvents/1.

The following steps will demonstrate this feature:

Step 1: Add these codes to the view:

Add a table that will display all events for the 'Local Events' to the user.

```
<table class="table table=striped">
  <thead>
  <tr><th>#</th><th>Local Events</th><th>Description</th><th></th>
  </tr></thead>
  <tbody>
```

Add a table row that will be used to show the event "Halloween Parade". To do this, modify the href tag to Local/1. When a user clicks on this link, the application will pass the route as well as the parameter '1' in the URL.

```
<tr>
    <td>1</td><td>1</td><td>Halloween Parade</td>
    <td><a href="#!Local/1">Event Details</a></td>
</tr>
```

Add a table row that will show the event "Cookfest". To do this, modify the href tag and replace it with "Local/2". When a user clicks on this link, the application will pass the route and the parameter '2' in the URL.

```
<tr>
    <td>2</td><td>2</td><td>Cookfest</td>
    <td><a href="#!Local/2">Event Details</a></td>
</tr>
```

Add a table row that will show the event "Dragon Boat Festival". To do this, change the href tag to "Halloween/3". When a user clicks on this option, the application will pass the route and the parameter '3' in the URL.

```
<tr>
    <td>3</td><td>3</td><td>Dragon Boat Festival</td>
    <td><a href="#!Local/3">Event Details</a></td>
</tr>
</tbody>
</table>
```

Step 2: Add :eventID after Local inside the $routeProvider function. This will assign all parameters passed to the eventID variable.

```
<div ng-view=""></div>
<script>
var app = angular.module("myApp", ["ngRoute"]);
app.config(function($routeProvider) {
    $routeProvider
    .when('/Local/:eventId', {
        templateUrl : "Local.html",
        controller : "localController"
    })
});
```

Step 3: Add the following codes to the controller:

```
app.controller('localController', function($scope, $routeParams) {
    $scope.localid=$routeParams.eventId;
});
```

The $routeParams should be added as a parameter in the controller function definition. It will provide access to any parameter that your application will pass in the URL.

The eventID should be passed as a route parameter within "routeParams" parameter. You will have to attach $routeParams.eventId variable to the scope object by assigning it as the value for $scope.localid. This will now allow you to reference the variable in the View through the member variable localid.

Step 5: Use an expression to show the eventid variable in the Local.html page.

Your Local.html template may contain the following;

```
<h1>Local Events</h1>
```

```
<br><br>{{localid}}
```

If you put together the above pieces of code, here's how the entire code will look:

```
<!DOCTYPE html>
<html>
<script
src="https://ajax.googleapis.com/ajax/libs/angularjs/1.6.4/angular.min.js">
</script>
<script src="https://ajax.googleapis.com/ajax/libs/angularjs/1.6.4/angular-
route.js"></script>

<body ng-app="myApp">
<h1>Events Calendar</h1>
<table class="table table=striped">
    <thead>
    <tr><th>#</th><th>Local Events</th><th>Description</th><th></th>
    </tr></thead>
    <tbody>
    <tr>
        <td>1</td><td>1</td><td>Halloween Parade</td>
        <td><a href="#!Local/1">Event Details</a></td>
    </tr>
    <tr>
        <td>2</td><td>2</td><td>Cookfest</td>
        <td><a href="#!Local/2">Event Details</a></td>
    </tr>
    <tr>
        <td>3</td><td>3</td><td>Dragon Boat Festival</td>
        <td><a href="#!Local/3">Event Details</a></td>
    </tr>
    </tbody>
</table>
<div ng-view=""></div>
<script>
var app = angular.module("myApp", ["ngRoute"]);
app.config(function($routeProvider) {
    $routeProvider
    .when('/Local/:eventId', {
        templateUrl : "Local.html",
        controller : "localController"
    })
});
app.controller('localController', function($scope, $routeParams) {
    $scope.localid=$routeParams.eventId;
});
</script>
</body>
</html>
```

If you execute the code, the web browser will display this page:

If you click on the Event Details link for the first event, here's what you will see on the browser:

When you clicked on the link for the first event, notice that '1', the event ID, was added to the URL. The AngularJS routeprovider service takes this number as a "routeparam" argument and assigns it to the scope object 'localid' which makes it accessible to the controller.

If you click on the Event Details link for the second event, here's what the browser will display:

Events Calendar

# Local Events	Description	
1 1	Halloween Parade	Event Details
2 2	Cookfest	Event Details
3 3	Dragon Boat Festival	Event Details

Local Events

2

If you click on the Event Details link for the third event, here's what you will see on the browser:

Events Calendar

# Local Events	Description	
1 1	Halloween Parade	Event Details
2 2	Cookfest	Event Details
3 3	Dragon Boat Festival	Event Details

Local Events

3

USING THE ANGULAR $ROUTE SERVICE

The $route service is used to access the route's properties. You can use it as an argument if this function was defined within the controller. Here's the syntax to make this available from the controller:

myApp.controller('MyController',function($scope,$route)

In the above statement, 'myApp' refers to the AngularJS module you have defined for the application. The 'MyController' refers to the controller you have created for the application. The function which was declared within the controller takes the $scope and $route as its parameters. You have learned that the $scope variable is used to pass data to the view. The $route parameter, on the other hand, provides access to the route's properties.

The following example will use the mainpage.html file in the previous section to demonstrate the use of the $route service.

In this example, you will have to create a custom variable and name it "newtext". It will store the string "My Events Calendar". You will bind this variable to the route. Next, you'll use the $route service to access the string from the controller. Finally, you will display the string in the View using the scope object.

Following are the specific steps that you have to perform:

Step 1: Create a key-value pair within the $routeProvider function. This is where you're going to add a key named newtext with a corresponding value of "My Events Calendar".

```
app.config(function($routeProvider) {
    $routeProvider
    .when('/Local/:eventId', {
        newtext:"My Events Calendar",
        templateUrl : "Local.html",
        controller : "localController"
    })
});
```

Step 2: Add these lines of code to the controller:

```
app.controller('localController', function($scope, $routeParams, $route) {
    $scope.localid=$routeParams.eventId;
    $scope.ntext=$route.current.newtext;
});
```

The controller function should include $route as one of the parameters. This will allow access to the route's properties.

Access the "newtext" variable by referencing "newtext" through the $route.current then assign it to the scope object's 'ntext' variable. This will provide access to the text variable from the View.

Here's how the entire code may appear:

```
<!DOCTYPE html>
<html>
<script
src="https://ajax.googleapis.com/ajax/libs/angularjs/1.6.4/angular.min.js">
</script>
<script src="https://ajax.googleapis.com/ajax/libs/angularjs/1.6.4/angular-
route.js"></script>

<body ng-app="myApp">
<h1>Events Calendar</h1>
<table class="table table=striped">
    <thead>
    <tr><th>#</th><th>Local Events</th><th>Description</th><th></th>
    </tr></thead>
    <tbody>
    <tr>
        <td>1</td><td>1</td><td>Halloween Parade</td>
        <td><a href="#!Local/1">Event Details</a></td>
    </tr>
     <tr>
        <td>2</td><td>2</td><td>Cookfest</td>
        <td><a href="#!Local/2">Event Details</a></td>
    </tr>
    <tr>
        <td>3</td><td>3</td><td>Dragon Boat Festival</td>
        <td><a href="#!Local/3">Event Details</a></td>
    </tr>
    </tbody>

</table>
<div ng-view=""></div>
<script>
var app = angular.module("myApp", ["ngRoute"]);
app.config(function($routeProvider) {
    $routeProvider
    .when('/Local/:eventId', {
        newtext:'My Events Calendar',
        templateUrl : "Local.html",
        controller : "localController"
    })
});
app.controller('localController', function($scope, $routeParams, $route) {
    $scope.localid=$routeParams.eventId;
    $scope.ntext=$route.current.newtext;
});
</script>
</body>
</html>
```

Step 3: Add an expression that will link the value of the 'ntext' variable to the Local.html page. This will allow the 'My Events Calendar' string to be displayed in the View.

The Local.html template may contain the following statements:

```
<h1>Local Events</h1>
```

```
<br><br>{{ntext}}
```

```
<br><br>{{localid}}
```

The View will display the string "My Events Calendar" as well as the event id when you click on one of the links.

If you run the code, here's what the web browser will display:

If you click on the Event Details link for the #1 event, the output will be:

The output indicates that the browser displays the string "My Events Calendar" along with the event ID when you click on one of the links.

ENABLING HTML5 ROUTING

AngularJS routes URLs with a hashtag # by default. For example, a typical URL that uses Angular routing would be:

http://mysite.com/#/about

To remove the hashtag and create a clean URL, you can use HTML5 routing. Using HTML5 routing will result in the following URL:

http://mysite.com/

Using HTML5 routing is otherwise known as displaying a pretty URL.

To implement HTML5 routing, you will need to perform two general steps:

- Configure the $locationProvider
- Set the base for relative links

The example in the previous section will be used to demonstrate HTM5 routing but the file will be renamed Sample.html for this purpose.

Here are the specific steps that you will perform to enable HTML5 routing:

Step 1: Add the required code to the module.

Add the $locationProvider service and set HTML5Mode to true:

```
var app = angular.module("myApp", ["ngRoute"]);
app.config(function($routeProvider, $locationProvider) {
    $routeProvider
    .when('/Local/:eventId', {
        newtext:'My Events Calendar',
        templateUrl : "Local.html",
        controller : "localController"
    })
    $locationProvider.html5Mode(true);
});
```

Step 2: Add a <base> within the <head> section of the HTML document. This will allow you to use relative links in your application.

```
<head>
<base href="/">
</head>
```

Step 3: To create clean and readable URLs, remove the hashtag (#) on all links:

```
<tr>
    <td>1</td><td>1</td><td>Halloween Parade</td>
    <td><a href="Local/1">Event Details</a></td>
</tr>
 <tr>
    <td>2</td><td>2</td><td>Cookfest</td>
    <td><a href="Local/2">Event Details</a></td>
</tr>
<tr>
    <td>3</td><td>3</td><td>Dragon Boat Festival</td>
    <td><a href="Local/3">Event Details</a></td>
</tr>
```

Here's how the entire code will look:

```
<!DOCTYPE html>
<html>
<script
src="https://ajax.googleapis.com/ajax/libs/angularjs/1.6.4/angular.min.js">
</script>
<script src="https://ajax.googleapis.com/ajax/libs/angularjs/1.6.4/angular-
route.js"></script>
<head>
<base href="/">
</head>
<body ng-app="myApp">
<h1>Events Calendar</h1>
<table class="table table=striped">
    <thead>
    <tr><th>#</th><th>Local Events</th><th>Description</th><th></th>
    </tr></thead>
    <tbody>
    <tr>
        <td>1</td><td>1</td><td>Halloween Parade</td>
        <td><a href="Local/1">Event Details</a></td>
    </tr>
     <tr>
        <td>2</td><td>2</td><td>Cookfest</td>
        <td><a href="Local/2">Event Details</a></td>
    </tr>
    <tr>
        <td>3</td><td>3</td><td>Dragon Boat Festival</td>
        <td><a href="Local/3">Event Details</a></td>
    </tr>
    </tbody>
</table>
<div ng-view=""></div>
<script>
var app = angular.module("myApp", ["ngRoute"]);
app.config(function($routeProvider, $locationProvider) {
    $routeProvider
    .when('/Local/:eventId', {
        newtext:'My Events Calendar',
        templateUrl : "Local.html",
        controller : "localController"
    })
    $locationProvider.html5Mode(true);
});
app.controller('localController', function($scope, $routeParams, $route) {
    $scope.localid=$routeParams.eventId;
    $scope.ntext=$route.current.newtext;
});
</script>
</body>
</html>
```

When you run the code and click on the Event Details for the #1 event, here's what the browser will display:

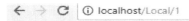

← → C ⓘ localhost/Local/1

Events Calendar

# Local Events	Description	
1 1	Halloween Parade	Event Details
2 2	Cookfest	Event Details
3 3	Dragon Boat Festival	Event Details

Local Events

My Events Calendar

1

Notice that the hash tag # has been removed from the address bar.

Summary:

Routing is the main feature used in implementing the concept of single page applications. Routing allows an application to display different views on a single web page.

AngularJS lets you set up a default route to specify the default view that will be displayed to users.

You can pass parameters to the route through the URL. To access these parameters, you will use the $routeParams parameter.

You can use the $route service to specify key-value pairs that can be injected in the View.

HTML5 is used to create clean and pretty URLS without the hash tag # symbol used in Angular routing.

CHAPTER 16: ANGULAR TABLES

Tables are among the most commonly used elements in HTML. They are created and designed in HTML using the following tags:

<tabl> This tag is the primary tag that you will use to display a table.
<tr>   This tag is used to segregate table rows.
<td>   This tag is used to display table data from the table.
<th>   This is used to specify data for the table header.

Using AngularJS with the above tags will make it easier to fill in table data.

In this chapter, you will learn how to populate table data with AngularJS using the ng-repeat directive. You will also see how the 'orderby' an 'uppercase' filters can be used with the $index property to show table indexes in AngularJs.

DISPLAYING TABLE DATA

When creating tables for web pages, you will be using the same HTML tags that you would normally use to create a table structure. This time, however, you will use the AngulJS ng-repeat directive to populate the data.

The following example will show you how to implement Angular tables. With this code, you will create an Angular table that contains subjects and their descriptions. Here are the specific steps to accomplish this objective:

Step 1: You will have to specify a style tag to the HTML page to enable the application to display the information as a table. This follows the usual procedure of adding formatting properties required by HTML elements. In this code, you will add two style values to the table. One style specifies a solid border for the table and the other defines padding for the table data. Here's what the code might be:

```
<!DOCTYPE html>
<html>
<script src="https://ajax.googleapis.com/ajax/libs/angularjs/
   1.6.4/angular.min.js"></script>
<head>
<meta charset="UTF-8">
<title>Events Description</title>
<style>
   table, th, td {border: 1px solid grey;
      padding: 10px;)
</style>
```

Step 2: Create the code that will generate the table and the data stored in the table.

```
<body>
<h1>Events Calendar</h1>
<div ng-app="sampleApp" ng-controller="localController">
   <table>
   <tr ng-repeat="item in event">
      <td>{{item.Name}}</td>
      <td>{{item.Description}}</td>
   </tr>
   </table>
</div>
<script>
var app = angular.module('sampleApp', []);
```

```
app.controller('localController', function($scope) {
    $scope.event = [
    {Name: "Halloween Parade", Description:"kiddie costume parade"},
    {Name: "Cookfest", Description:"cooking contest"},
    {Name: "Dragon Boat Festival", Description:"boat race"}
    ]
});
```

How the Code Works:

The code creates a member variable named 'event' and assigns an array with three key value pairs to the event variable. The array elements will be used as data when the table is displayed. It also assigns the 'event' variable to the scope object. This will make it accessible from the View.

The <table> tag is used to create a table.

The 'ng-repeat' directive was used for each data row. This directive uses the variable 'item' to go through all the key-value pairs specified in the course scope object.

The <td> tag is used to display table data.

Here's the whole code:

```
<!DOCTYPE html>
<html>
<script
src="https://ajax.googleapis.com/ajax/libs/angularjs/1.6.4/angular.min.js">
</script>
<head>
<meta charset="UTF-8">
<title>Events Description</title>
<style>
    table, th, td {border: 1px solid grey;
        padding: 10px;)
</style>
</head>
<body>
<h1>Events Calendar</h1>
<div ng-app="sampleApp" ng-controller="localController">
    <table>
    <tr ng-repeat="item in event">
        <td>{{item.Name}}</td>
        <td>{{item.Description}}</td>
    </tr>
    </table>
</div>
<script>
var app = angular.module('sampleApp', []);
app.controller('localController', function($scope) {
    $scope.event = [
    {Name: "Halloween Parade", Description:"kiddie costume parade"},
    {Name: "Cookfest", Description:"cooking contest"},
    {Name: "Dragon Boat Festival", Description:"boat race"}
    ]
});
</script>
</body>
</html>
```

If you run the code, here's what the browser will display:

Halloween Parade	kiddie costume parade
Cookfest	cooking contest
Dragon Boat Festival	boat race

Notice that the browser displayed the table as specified and that the key-value pairs defined within the localController were used to populate the table. The ng-repeat directive was used to generate the table data.

USING ORDERBY AND UPPERCASE FILTER TO DISPLAY TABLE DATA

Built-in filters are commonly used to modify how table data is displayed to users. The 'uppercase' filter, for example, is used to format and display all elements of the output string in uppercase.

This section will discuss how you can use the uppercase and orderBy filters in tables to change the way the browser displays table data. You will use the code that created the Event Calendar table.

OrderBy Filter

The OrderBy filter lets you sort a table using one column as index. For example, here's the output of the Events Calendar table data:

Halloween Parade	kiddie costume parade
Cookfest	cooking contest
Dragon Boat Festival	boat race

Notice that the table data were arranged randomly. You may want to present them in alphabetical order based on the data stored in one of the columns.

The following statement applies the 'orderBy' filter to sort table data and specifies the first column as the sort index within the ng-repeat directive:

```
<tr ng-repeat="item in event | orderBy:'Name'">
```

If you execute the code, here's what the browser will display:

Events Calendar

Cookfest	cooking contest
Dragon Boat Festival	boat race
Halloween Parade	kiddie costume parade

The output shows that the table data had been arranged in an ascending order based on the first column data.

How the Code Works:

The code practically uses the same statements to create the table but this time, it uses the ng-repeat directive with the 'orderBy' filter to specify that the data should be ordered based on the 'Name' key.

Uppercase Filter

The uppercase filter is used to convert the table data to uppercase.

To demonstrate, you can present the first column, Name, in uppercase by using the pipe symbol (|) and the uppercase filter within the ng-repeat directive. Here's the statement:

```
<tr ng-repeat="item in event">
    <td>{{item.Name | uppercase}}</td>
    <td>{{item.Description}}</td>
```

If you run the code, this will be the output:

Events Calendar

HALLOWEEN PARADE	kiddie costume parade
COOKFEST	cooking contest
DRAGON BOAT FESTIVAL	boat race

The use of the 'uppercase' filter caused the first column data to be presented in uppercase letters.

How the Code Works:

It used the same code as the previous example to create the table. This time, however, the 'uppercase' filter was used in combination with the 'item.Name' variable inside the ng-repeat block.

DISPLAYING TABLE INDEX

Sometimes, you may want to include an index to make table data more readable. You can do this in AngularJS by adding a <td> tag with $index.

Using the same example to create a table, you can add an index by inserting the following statement within the ng-repeat block:

```
<td>{{$index + 1}}</td>
```

Here's the ng-repeat block at this point:

```
<tr ng-repeat="item in event">
    <td>{{$index + 1}}</td>
    <td>{{item.Name}}</td>
    <td>{{item.Description}}</td>
</tr>
```

If you run the code, here's what the output will be:

Events Calendar

1	Halloween Parade	kiddie costume parade
2	Cookfest	cooking contest
3	Dragon Boat Festival	boat race

The use of the $index attribute created a new column on the table. This column displays the index for each row in increments of 1.

How the Code Works

To add another column that will show the index number, the code used the $index property with the +1 operator.

Summary:

Angular tables are created using standard HTML tags.
The ng-repeat directive is used to populate table data.
You can display text-based columns in uppercase by using the uppercase filter.
You can sort a table by using the orderBy filter.
The '$index' attribute is used to build a table index.

CHAPTER 17: VALIDATION

Validation is the process of verifying and ensuring the accuracy and completeness of data.

A site that requires a user to complete a form before allowing the user to access the site would normally provide input fields where users can enter their email id, username, password, or other information. A validation process is typically performed when the user submits the form.

Client-side validation will ensure that the data required are entered correctly before they are sent to the server. Combining client-side validation with server-side validation will help ensure the efficiency and security of your web applications.

For instance, if an input field requires an email address, it will have to be entered in the format name@site.domain. Validation will fail if the user enters another format.

SUBMITTING A FORM

The submit event typically handles the process of sending the information entered by a user on a web page. To complement this, AngularJS provides the ng-submit directive which is used to attach the application to the browser's submit event. This directive will allow you to perform several processes inside the controller relative to the submit event and present the processed data to users.

The following example will display a textbox to users where they can enter the event that they want to learn more about. The page will contain a submit button which, when clicked, will add an event to a list.

```
<!DOCTYPE html>
<html>
<script
src="https://ajax.googleapis.com/ajax/libs/angularjs/1.6.4/angular.min.js">
</script>
<head>
<meta charset="UTF-8">
</head>
<body>
<div ng-app="newApp" ng-controller="localController">
<form ng-submit="Display()">
Enter an event that you would like to attend
<input type="text" ng-model="Event"><br>
<input type="submit" value="Submit"/>
<ul ng-repeat="item in AllEvent">
    <li>{{item}}</li>
</ul>
</form>
</div>
    <script>
        var newApp = angular.module('newApp',[]);
        newApp.controller('localController', function($scope) {
            $scope.AllEvent=[];
            $scope.Display = function()
            {
                $scope.AllEvent.push($scope.Event);

            }
        });
    </script>
</body>
</html>
```

Here's what the code does:

<form ng-submit="Display()">
Enter an event that you would like to attend
<input type="text" ng-model="Event">

The code declares the HTML <form> tag which will store the control for the "submit button" and "textbox". The ng-submit directive is then used to attach the "Display()" function to the form. This function is added to the controller and will be called once the user submits the form.

```
<input type="text" ng-model="Event"><br>
```

The above statement binds the "text" field to the "Event" variable. It specifies a text control where users can enter the event they want to join. It will be attached to the 'Event' variable in the controller.

```
<input type="submit" value="Submit"/>
```

The application specifies a submit button that a user can click after entering the name of an event.

```
<ul ng-repeat="item in AllEvent">
  <li>{{item}}</li>
</ul>
```

The ng-repeat directive was used to show a list of events that the user will enter. This directive runs through each event in the 'AllEvent' array and shows the corresponding event name.

```
var newApp = angular.module('newApp',[]);
newApp.controller('localController', function($scope) {
    $scope.AllEvent=[];
```

The above block declares and initializes the 'AllEvent' array within the 'localController'. It will store all events that the user will enter.

```
$scope.Display = function()
{
```

The above statement defines the Display() function. This function will be invoked whenever the user clicks on the submit button.

```
{
     $scope.AllEvent.push($scope.Event);
}
```

The application uses the push array function to add the events that a user may enter into the 'AllEvent' array through the 'Event' variable.

If you run the code, here's what the browser will display:

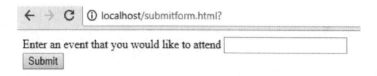

If you enter the event "Carnival" on the textbox and click on the 'Submit' button, this will be the output:

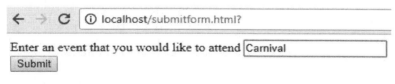

- Carnival

The item you have entered in the textbox was displayed on the list. Clicking on the 'Submit' button invokes the Display() function and causes the entered text to be displayed as a list type.

Type another event on the textbox, "Thanksgiving", and click on the 'Submit' button. Here's the output:

← → C ⓘ localhost/submitform.html?

Enter an event that you would like to attend [Thanksgiving   ]
[Submit]

- Carnival

- Thanksgiving

The last event you entered was added to the list of events.

The Display() function appends the string to the 'AllEvent' array variable. The ng-repeat directive runs through the array's values and shows them as list values.

USING HTML5 FOR FORM VALIDATION

Form validation involves pre-validating form input data before they reach the server. Validating information on the client side is a good practice because it will mean less overhead when the user enters incorrect information.

The following example will show how form validation is done in HTML5:

This application will display a registration form where users are required to enter details such as username, age, email, and password. It will include a form which will contain validation controls to make sure that users will enter the required data properly. Here's the form section. You can add it to the standard heading and bottom sections of an HTML page.

```html
<form>
Enter your username:
<input type="text" name="username" required><br><br>

Enter your password:   
<input type="password" /><br><br>

Enter your email address:
<input type="email" /><br><br>

Enter your age:          
<input type="number"/><br>
<br>         

<input type="submit" value="Submit"/>
</form>
```

Here are the key points of the example:

The 'required' property was applied to the text input type for username. It specifies that the textbox should contain some text and should not be empty when the user submits the form.

The second input type was specified as a 'password'. This means that any text entered by a user in this field will be masked.

The email attribute was assigned to the next input type. Hence, the text that would be entered in this field should match the name@site.domain email pattern.

The 'number' attribute was given to the last input type. This means that it will only take numeric inputs. It will not accept entries such as letters or symbols.

If you execute the code, the web browser will display the following form:

If you try to enter the form without entering anything, here's how the browser will respond:

The validation for the field marked as 'required' will fail if the user fails to enter a value in the textbox. Notice the error message asking the user to fill out the field.

The next field which was marked with the 'password' control will display the "*" symbol to mask the characters that the user will type on the password box. To see this in action, enter the username 'AJSstudent' and the password abc123 and click on 'Submit'. This is what you'll see on the web page as you type the password:

Enter your username: AJSstudent

Enter your password: ••••••

Enter your email address:

Enter your age:

Submit

The next field which was marked with the 'email' validation control will cause an error to be displayed if the user enters a value that does not correspond to the email address format. To test this control, enter an invalid email address 'example.com' and click the Submit button. Here's what you'll see on the web page:

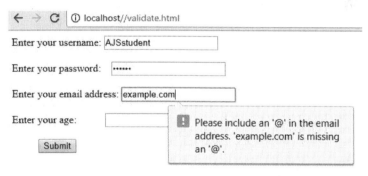

The email validation control caused the error pop-up to appear on the page.

Finally, you can test the validation control for the last field by entering the character 'ax':

Because you have set the field as a 'number' field, it will not accept characters as input.

USING ANGULARJS FOR FORM VALIDATION

AngularJS has several properties that you can use to validate forms. Following are possible states of the form which can be specified as either true or false:

$pristine   The user has not modified any field.
$dirty   The user has modified one or more field.
$valid   The content of a field is valid.
$invalid   The content of a field is not valid.
$submitted   The form has been submitted.

The above controls can be used to display relevant messages to the user. For example, when a user fails to provide data to a required field, the web page should give a warning message to the user.

Here are the steps that you have to follow to perform AngularJS validation:

Step 1: Specify the no validate attribute when you declare the form. This tells HTML5 that AngularJS will take over the validation process.

Step 2: Make sure that a name had been defined for the form. This is necessary because the form name will be referenced during Angular validation.

Step 3: Make sure that a name had been defined for each control. This is important because references will have to be made to the control name during AngularJS validation.

Step 4) Check for the occurrence of the $valid, $invalid, and $dirty attributes for the controls using the ng-show directive.

The following example will demonstrate how you can perform AngularJS validation.

This simple code will present a textbox in which users can enter their username. A submit button is added to the page.

```
<html>
<script
src="https://ajax.googleapis.com/ajax/libs/angularjs/1.6.4/angular.min.js">
</script>
<head>
<meta charset="UTF-8">
</head>
<body>
<form ng-app="sampleApp" ng-controller="sampleController" name="myForm"
novalidate>

    <p>Username:<br>
        <input type="text" name="user" ng-model="user" required>
<span style="color:red" ng-show="myForm.user.$dirty &&
myForm.user.$invalid">
<span ng-show="myForm.user.$error.required">Username is required.</span>
</span>
    </p><p>
        <input type="submit"
            ng-disabled="myForm.user.$dirty && myForm.user.$invalid">
    </p></form><script>
        var app=angular.module('sampleApp', []);
        app.controller('sampleController', function($scope) {
            $scope.user='AJSstudent';
        });
    </script>
</body>
</html>
```

What the code does:

The name 'myForm' was given to the Form. You will need this to access the form controls for Angular validation.

The 'novalidate' property was used to ensure that AngularJS will be allowed to perform the validation on the HTML form.

The ng-show directive was used to look for the $invalid and $dirty attributes. If the textbox value is null, the $invalid attribute becomes true. Similarly, if the user had interacted with the textbox, the $dirty attribute becomes true. When both attributes are true, the validation fails. This also means that ng-show will be true causing it to display the corresponding span control.

The code enables the $error attribute on the required field which will become true if no data was entered for the field. If no value was entered on the required textbox, the string "Username is required" will be displayed.

When the textbox value is not valid, you may want prevent the user from clicking on the submit button. To do this, you can use the 'ng-disabled' attribute to set up the controls to act based on the values of the $invalid and $dirty properties. The example uses the ng-disabled property to disable the Submit button based on the values of these two properties.

The code sets the initial value of the textbox. In this case, it will show the text 'AJSstudent' when the form is displayed:

At this point, you can see that the 'submit button' is enabled. If you try to remove the default text 'AJSstudent' from the textbox, the page will display the validation error message and disable the 'Submit button':

USING ANGULARJS AUTO VALIDATE

AngularJS offers a functionality that will allow you to automatically validate all form controls without writing a custom code. You can access this facility by including the module "jcs-AutoValidate" in your code.

The JCS-AutoValidate custom module handles the validation and display of error message and eliminates the use of special code.

The following example will demonstrate how you can use this module:

```
<!DOCTYPE html>
<html>
<script
src="https://ajax.googleapis.com/ajax/libs/angularjs/1.6.4/angular.min.js">
</script>
<script src="https://cdn.rawgit.com/jonsamwell/angular-auto-
validate/master/dist/jcs-auto-validate.min.js"></script>
<body>
<h1>Event Registration</h1>
<div ng-app="sampleApp">
<div class="form-group">
<form name="myForm" novalidate>
    <p>Username<br>
    <div class="form-group">
<input class="form-control" type="text" id="user" ng-model="user"
required="required">
</div>
    <div><div class="form-group">
    <input type="submit"></div>
</div>
</form>
</div>
</div>
<script>
    var app=angular.module('sampleApp',['jcs-autoValidate']);
</script>
</body>
</html>
```

The form has a textbox control which is designated as a required field. If the user does enter a value on this field, the application will display an error message.

How the code works:

You have to add a reference to the 'jcs-auto-validate.js' script which contains the auto validation functionality.

You need to ensure that all elements are placed inside a 'form-group' class. That includes HTML elements such as span control, input control, and div control.

Add the jcs-autovalidate as a dependency in the Angular module.
If you run the code, this will be the initial output:

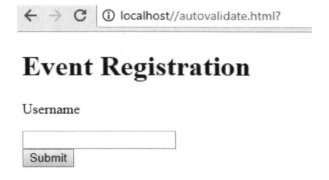

If you try to submit the form without entering a text, this will cause a pop up error message to appear:

USING LADDA BUTTONS

Ladda buttons allows you to provide a visual effect to buttons when they are clicked/pressed by users. It is a special framework made specifically to handle buttons.

A button with a 'ladda' attribute displays a spin effect when clicked. It also offers other button styles that will allow you to show other visual effects.

The following example will illustrate a 'ladda' button in action. The code will use a basic form with a submit button. When the user clicks the button, it will display a spin effect.

```
<body>
<h1>Event Registration</h1>
<div ng-app="sampleApp" ng-controller="sampleController">
<div class="form-group">
<form name="myForm" novalidate ng-submit="submit()">
<div>
    <div class="form-group">

        <button class="btn btn-primary" type="submit" ladda="submitting"
name="sbutton"
            data-style="expand-right">Submit</button>
</div></div>
</form>
</div></div>
<script>
    var app=angular.module('sampleApp',['jcs-autoValidate','angular-
ladda']);
    app.controller('sampleController', function($scope) {
        $scope.submitting=false;
        $scope.submit=function() {
            $scope.submitting=true;
        }
    });
</script>
</body>
</html>
```

How the Code Works

The code invokes the "submit" function using the ng-submit directive. You will need this function to modify the submit button's ladda attribute, a special property.

The ladda framework will only work if you add the AngularJS-ladda module to the AngularJS application.

This statement sets the variable 'submitting' as the value of the ladda property:

```
<button class="btn btn-primary" type="submit"
    ladda="submitting" name="sbutton"
```

The ladda framework also offers the data-style property which allows you to add more visual effects.

The initial value of the 'submitting' variable was set to false:

```
app.controller('sampleController', function($scope) {
    $scope.submitting=false;
```

This sets the ladda attribute to false. This means that initially, the ladda effect will not be implemented.

The following statement declares a function that will be invoked when the user clicks on the submit button:

```
$scope.submit=function() {
        $scope.submitting=true;
    }
```

This time, the value of the 'submitting' variable was set to 'true'. This means that the 'ladda' effect will be implemented on the submit button.

Chapter Summary:

The ng-submit directive handles the processing of form data entered and submitted by users.

The 'required' attribute is used to validate textbox HTML controls.

HTML provides additional controls such as number, email, and password which have their own validation set.

AngularJS implements form validation by checking the form control's $pristine, $dirty, $invalid, and $valid values.

The JCS-autovalidate module can be used to implement auto validation in Angular applications.

You can add ladda buttons to an Angular application to enhance the visual effects when a button is clicked.

CHAPTER 18: HTTP AND AJAX

AJAX stands for Asynchronous JavaScript and XML. It is a client-side script that facilitates data exchange with the server and the updating of a web page without completely refreshing the page.

Many web applications use AJAX as a method for retrieving server data and reloading web pages. It offers several benefits:

AJAX minimizes network utilization and helps make operations more efficient by performing callbacks and sending only the required files to the server.

It lets you perform asynchronous calls to the server. This allows partial updating of a web page without actually refreshing the entire page.

AJAX can enhance the performance, speed, and usability of web applications.

By eliminating page postback, applications that utilize AJAX are more user-friendly and responsive.

HIGH LEVEL INTERACTIONS WITH THE SERVER

AngularJS offers two Application Program Interfaces (APIs) for handling AJAX requests:

$resource
$http

The $resource property facilitates high level interactions with web servers.

High level interaction means that the concerns are limited to the type of functionality that a server offers. It is not concerned about the details of what the server actually does regarding the functionality.

REST-based Architecture

REST, or Representational State Transfer, is a commonly used architecture in most modern web-based systems. This type lets you use the normal GET, PUT, DELETE, and POST HTTP verbs when working with web-based applications.

For example, here's an application that keeps a list of courses. If you need the list of all courses, you can do the following:

You can set the application to expose a URL like http://example/courses.

If the application is based on the REST architecture, you can use the HTTP verb 'GET' to fetch the complete list of courses from the URL http://example/courses.

For instance, if one of the Courses has an ID of 101, you can obtain information about this course though the URL http//example/courses/101.

$resource object

Angular's $resource object can be used to work with servers using REST-based structure.

Here's the syntax for the resource statement:

```
var resource Object = $resource(url);
```

Once the resourceObject is available, you will have access to some special functions. These functions will let you make REST calls.

Here are the functions and their usage:

get([params], [success], [error])
You can use this function to make the standard GET call.

query([params], [success], [error])
You can also use this function to make the standard GET. Its response will include an array.

save([params], postData, [success], [error])
This function can be called to make a standard POST call.

remove([params], postData, [success], [error])
You can use this function to make a standard DELETE call.

Notice that all functions used the parameter 'params' to supply the required parameters.

For example, assuming the value of Course: 'AngularJS' was passed as a 'param' with this code:

get('http://example/courses' ,'{ Course: 'AngularJS' }').

It will invoke the URL
http://example/course?Course=AngularJS as a component of the get() function.

Using the $resource property

To use the $resource property, you'll have to follow these steps:

Step 1: Download the 'angular-resource.js' file from AngularJS.com. Next, this file should be inserted it in the application.

Step 2: To use the $resource, a dependency will have to be declared on the 'ngResource' module. The declaration will have to be performed on the application module.

The following code calls the 'ngResource' module from the MyApp application:

```
angular.module(MyApp,['ngResource']); //MyApp is the main module
```

Step 3: Call the $resource() function through the REST endpoint.

Doing this gives the $resource object the capability to call the required functionality which the REST endpoint will expose.

This code invokes the endpoint URL http://example/courses/101:

```
angular.module('MyApp.services').factory('Entry',
function($resource)
{
    return $resource('/example/Courses/:101);
});
```

The above example does the following:

In the module definition, the statement 'MyApp.services' creates a service. Here, the name of the AngularJS application is 'MyApp'.

The factory method was used to generate the objects of the service. The name 'Entry' was given to the service but you can choose another name that you think will be more appropriate. The service creates a function that will invoke the $resource api.

You will need the $resource() function to invoke a REST endpoint. The following example uses the URL as the REST endpoint:

$resource('/example/Courses/:101)

The REST endpoint indicates that an application named 'Courses' is stored on the main website 'example'. This application was created with the use of a REST-based structure.

A resource class object is created, and it will contain the functions remove(), query(), delete(), save(), and get().

Step 4: You're now ready to use the methods remove (), query (), delete (), save (), and get () in your controller.

The example below uses the get () function:

```
angular.module('MyApp.controllers',[]);
angular.module('MyApp.controllers').controller('MyAppController',function($scope, MyFunction) {
  var obj = MyFunction.get({ 1: $scope.id }, function() {
    console.log(obj);
  });
```

How the code works:

A GET request to /example/Courses/:101 will be issued by the get () function.

Within the URL, the $scope.id will replace parameter 101.

The get () function is expected to return null that will be filled automatically. The servers will send the data.

Once the data arrives the get ( ) function takes a second argument, a callback, that will be executed. The output may be a JSON object that will return a list of Courses that were exposed from the site.

FETCHING DATA FROM MYSQL AND SQL DATABASE SERVER

You can also use AngularJS to fetch data from a MySQL or SQL server.

If you're using Asp.Net to connect to an MS SQL database or PHP to connect to a MySQL database, you'll have to make sure that the data are rendered in JSON format.

For example, assuming that a PHP site is serving data from a database server, here's what should happen:

Step 1: Ensure that PHP fetches data from the database server and serves them in JSON format.

Step 2: Write a code that uses the $http service to fetch the JSON data.

The following AngularJS code uses the $http service to obtain specified information from the server:

```
<script>
var app = angular.module('myApp', []);
app.controller('localCtrl', function($scope, $http) {
   $http.get("http://example/local/getEvents.PHP")
   .then(function(response)
{
      $scope.events = response.data.records;});
});
</script>
```

Step 3: Use the ng-repeat directive to display the data in the View.

The following examples uses the ng-repeat directive to run though all key-value pairs in the JSON object generated by applying the "get" method:

```
<div ng-app="myApp" ng-controller="AngularCtrl">
<table>
  <tr ng-repeat="item in topics">
   <td>{{ item.Name }}</td>
   <td>{{ item.Description }}</td>
  </tr>
</table>
</div>
```

The above code displays the key, "Name", and its value, "Description", for each JSON object.

Summary:

The $resource object is used to interact with REST applications at the high level.

The $http service can be used to fetch data from web applications. It can interact with web applications on a more detailed level.

The $http service can be used to fetch data from a MySQL/MS SQL database server through a PHP application. The ng-repeat directive is then used to render the data in a table format.

CHAPTER 19: USING NG-INCLUDE

Most programming languages support the distribution of functionalities across the different files of an application. This allows you to define a functionality or logic in a separate file. The functionality can then be accessed and used by different applications by including the file. This is the concept behind the 'Include' statement.

HTML doesn't automatically support including client-side code from external files. However, you can use some strategies that will allow you to include external files with HTML codes to the current HTML file.

CLIENT SIDE INCLUDES

Using Javascript is a common way to include HTML code in a file. JavaScript can be used to control HTML pages which make it a good tool for including code from separate files.

Here are the steps to achieve this:

Step 1: Create a file and save it as Ext.html with the following code:

```
<div>
    This    file    will    be
included.
<div>
```

Step 2: Create a file and save it as Mainfile.html. This will be the main application file and will contain the following code:

```html
<html>
    <head>
        <script src="//cdn.example.com/jquery.js"></script>
        <script>
        $(function(){
          $("#Content").load("Ext.html");
        });
    </script>
    </head>

    <body>
      <div id="Content"></div>
    </body>
</html>
```

Here are the notable sections of the above code:

The JavaScript function contains the statement '$("#Content").load ("Ext.html");'. This injects the Ext.html code to the <div> tag with an id of 'Content'.

The body contains a <div> tag with 'Content' as its specified id. That's how the Ext.html code will be included.

It references a jquery script. JQuery allows better control over HTML DOM.

SERVER SIDE INCLUDES

Server Side Includes can also be used to insert an external code throughout the entire website. It is generally performed when you want to insert content on the following sections of HTML documents:

Navigation menu
Page header
Page footer

The web server recognizes a Server Side Includes though the special extensions to the file names. Some of the common extensions are .cgi, .stm, .shtm, and .shtml.

The 'include' directive is used to include content. Following is an example of its usage:

```
<!--#include virtual="navigation.cgi" -->
```

The 'virtual' keyword specifies the target in relation to the application's domain root.

The use of the 'include' directive facilitates the insertion of a separate document to another document.

Additionally, you can also use the file parameters if you have to define the path relative to the current file's location.

The keyword 'virtual' needs to be used with the 'include' directive. Its parameter specifies the file that you want to include. The web server process should have sufficient rights to execute the script or read the file. Otherwise, the 'include' command will not succeed.

ANGULARJS INCLUDES

AngularJS provides the ng-include directive to facilitate the process of including functionality from external Angular files.

The 'ng-include' directive is primarily used to obtain and include an external HTML code to an AngularJS application.

The following example will demonstrate the use of the ng-include directive:

Step 1: Create a new file and name it Table.html. This will be the target file of the ng-include directive. That is, it is the external file that will be inserted to the main application. Write the following code:

```
<table>
<style>
  th, td {border: 1px solid grey;
    padding: 10px;)
</style>
  <tr ng-repeat="course in tutorial">
    <td>{{course.Name}}</td>
    <td>{{course.Description}}</td>
  </tr>
</table>
```

The code points to a scope variable named 'tutorial'. It uses ng-repeat to run through the courses stored in 'tutorial' and shows the corresponding values for 'Name' and 'Description'.

Step 2: Create the main application file and name it as Main.html. It is an AngularJS file with the following noteworthy features:

- It uses the 'ng-include' directive to inject the Table.html code.

- It creates a variable named 'tutorial' in the controller. This variable holds three key-value pairs which correspond to the following:

Name: This indicates the course title.
Description: This provides a short explanation for each course.

```html
<!DOCTYPE html>
<html>
<head>
    <meta charset="UTF-8">
    <title>Event Registration</title>
        <script
src="http://ajax.googleapis.com/ajax/libs/angularjs/1.6.4/angular.min.js">
</script>
</head>
<body ng-app="myApp">
<div ng-controller="courseController">
    <h3> Website Development Courses</h3>
                <div ng-include="'Table.html'"></div>
</div>
<script>

    var myApp = angular.module('myApp',[]);
    myApp.controller('courseController', function($scope) {
        $scope.tutorial =[
            {Name: "HTML5" , Description : "Structure of Web Pages"},
            {Name: "JavaScript" , Description : "Dynamic Web Pages"},
            {Name: "AngularJS" , Description : "Extending HTML Attributes"}
        ];

    });
</script>
</body>
</html>
```

If you execute the code, the browser will display the data in tabular format:

Chapter Summary:

Unlike other programming languages, HTML doesn't offer a direct way of embedding external HTML content.

The combination of JavaScript and JQuery is the most preferred option for including external HTML content.

The 'include' directive can be used with the 'virtual' parameter keyword to include HTML content from an external file. This method is called server-side includes.

AngularJS likewise allows the embedding of external HTML files to the current HTML file using the 'ng-include' directive.

CHAPTER 20: DEPENDENCY INJECTION

Dependency injection is a commonly used technique in software design. It is mostly identified with the inversion of control concept. In this concept, the main object does not create its own object but relies on an external source to produce the objects (dependencies). Injection is the process of passing objects or dependencies to a client or object that will use them.

In AngularJS, you can inject dependencies through the 'constructor function' or 'injectable factory method'. The 'value' and 'service' components can be passed as dependencies to these components. An example would be a code that uses $http service for fetching content from a MySQL/MS SQL database.

This code shows how you can define the $http service within the controller:

```
nyApp.controller ('AngularJSController', function ($scope, $http)
```

Defining the $http service in this manner establishes the controller's dependency on this service. When you run the code, AngularJS performs the following:

Since the controller is dependent on the "http service', AngularJS will have to ensure the availability of the service. Hence, it will verify if the service had been instantiated.

In case it had not been instantiated, AngularJS will have to call the 'factory' function. This will be used to create an $http object.

An instance of $http service will be made available to the controller through the AngularJS injector.

At this point, the dependency was already injected in the controller. You will now be ready to call the required functionality of the $http service.

There are two ways to implement Dependency injection in AngularJS:

- Through a "Service"
- Through the "Value" component

USING SERVICE

Service is a JavaScript object that is typically injected using AngularJS dependency mechanism. It consists of a set of functions that are aimed at performing a specific task.

An example would be the "$http" service. When injected, it will provide the following required functions:

get (), delete(), remove(), save(), query

Injecting the $http service will enable you to call the above functions from your controller.

In the following example, you will find out how to make your own service. This code will create a multiplication service that will multiply the values of x and y:

nyApp.controller ('AngularJSController', function ($scope, $http)

```
var mainApp = AngularJS.module("mainApp", []);
mainApp.service('MultiplicationService', function() {
  this.Multiplication = function(a,b) {
     return x*y;
  }
});
mainApp.controller('MultController', function ($scope, MultiplicationService) {

     $scope.result = MultiplicationService.Multiplication(2,8);
});
```

How the Code Works:

The following code uses the service parameter to create a new service called "MultiplicationService".

```
mainApp.service('MultiplicationService', function() {
```

The code below creates a new function named Multiplication within the service. This function takes 2 arguments, x and y. The Multiplication function will be accessible to the application once the MultiplicationService is instantiated.

```
this.Multiplication = function(a,b) {
```

This line defines the body of the Multiplication function. The function simply multiplies the arguments and returns the product.

```
return x*y;
```

This code shows how dependency is injected in the controller.

The code references the 'MultiplicationService' inside the controller definition. When it encounters this line, AngularJS will instantiate an object of 'MultiplicationService'.

```
mainApp.controller('MultController', function ($scope, MultiplicationService)
```

The following code accesses the 'Multiplication' function and assigns the function to the controller's $scope object:

```
$scope.result = MultiplicationService.Multiplication(2,8);
```

USING VALUE COMPONENT

The concept of using value component to inject dependency is based on the typical process of creating objects and passing them to the controller for processing.

In AngularJS, a value can be a string, number, or JavaScript object. Values are commonly injected into services, controllers, or factories. A value should be linked to a module. These examples demonstrate how values can be added to an AngularJS module:

```
var myApp = angular.module("myApp", []);

myApp.value("objectValue", { value1 : "def", value2 : 123} );
myApp.value("stringValue", "xyz");
myApp.value("numberValue", 123);
```

Injecting a Value

You can easily inject a value into a controller by adding the name of the value to the controller's function parameter. The value's name refers to the first parameter in the key-value pair that was passed to the value() function.

There are two important steps that you need to perform to implement this concept:

Step 1: Create an object though the value component and bind it to the main module. This value component accepts two arguments: a key and the object's value.

Step 2: Use the AngularJS Controller to access the JavaScript object.

The following example will demonstrate the above steps:

```
<div ng-app="sampleApp" ng-controller="eventController">
    <h1>Events Calendar</h1>
        {{number}}
</div>
<script>
    var sampleApp = angular.module("sampleApp", []);
    sampleApp.value("eventID", 123);
    sampleApp.controller('eventController', function($scope, eventID) {
        $scope.number=eventID;
    });
</script>
```

This line uses the value() function to define a key-value pair with eventID as the key and '123' as the value:

sampleApp.value ("eventID", 123);

This statement specifies the EventID as a function parameter and makes it accessible to the EventController:

sampleApp.controller('eventController', function($scope,eventID) {

This statement assigns the value of EventID to a variable of the $scope object named ID. This will allow the number 123, the value of eventID, to be passed to the View:

```
$scope.ID =eventID;
```

This statement passes the ID parameter to the View which will cause the value of '123' to be displayed on the webpage:

```
{{ID}}
```

Summary:

Dependency injection refers to the technique of injecting objects/functionality to a module.

The use of dependency injection supports code reusability.

You can use the value component of AngularJS for injecting a JavaScript object to a controller.
The service module lets you create reusable custom services.

CHAPTER 21: INTRODUCTION: TESTING WITH KARMA

The developers of AngularJS ensured that there would be ways to test the framework in its entirety. There are other options for testing but it is usually performed using Karma. It works brilliantly with AngularJS because it offers excellent functionality that is well suited to AngularJS codes.

You can perform separate tests for directives and controllers as well as carry out end to end testing.

This chapter will provide an introduction to Angular JS Karma testing and controller testing.

Introduction –Testing with Karma

Google's AngularJS team created Karma to automate testing of Angular codes. To use it, you will have to install it through NPM (Node Package Manager). Here are the steps for installing and configuring Karma:

Step 1: Run the statement via the following command line:

```
npm install karma karma-chrome-launcher karma-jasmine
```

The statement references three libraries:

karma-chrome-launcher: This is an independent library that allows Google's browser, Chrome, to recognize karma commands

Karma: Your code will be tested via the main library that will be used to test your code

karma-jasmine: Jasmine is a Karma-dependent framework.

Step 2: Install Karma command line utility.

This utility is needed to execute commands in karma. The karma environment will also be initialized using this same utility.

Run this statement:

"npm install karma-cli"

Step 3: Configure the Karma framework

Configuration is done by running the following command:

"karma–init"

After installing and configuring Karma, it will create a karma.conf.js file.

The configuration file relays the following information to the karma runtime engine:

- The application's name.
- It is dependent on AngularJS core modules
- The unit testing functionality from Angular.JS-mocks.js file should be used to test the application.
- That unit tests will be kept in the test folder

The process will also show you something like this snippet:

```
files: [
  'Your application Name'/AngularJS/AngularJS.js',
  'Your application Name'/AngularJS-mocks/AngularJS-mocks.js',
  'lib/app.js',
  'tests/*.js'
]
```

Testing Controllers

End-to-end testing is also supported by the Karma network and it can be used to test the $scope object and other controllers.

The following example will demonstrate how Controller testing is performed through Karma:

The first step is to create a controller definition. To do that, you need to do the following steps:

- Create an ID variable. Initialize its value to 10.
- This ID variable should then be assigned to the $scope object.

The next step is to test if the ID variable's value was set to 10 which will also verify the existence of its controller.

Before you start the testing, make sure that the following are installed and available:

Angular.JS-mocks library – You can install this mock library through npm. You can do that by running the following statement on the command line:

"npm install Angular JS-mocks"

You need to edit the karma.conf.js file. This will ensure that the test will include all the right files. The following example displays the file parts that need modification:

```
files: ['lib/AngularJS.js','lib/AngularJS-mocks.js',
    'lib/index.js','test/*.js']
```

The 'files' parameter is used to tell Karma the files required in the testing. In order to run Angular tests you will need the Angular.js and AngularJS=mocks.js.

The following code will be saved in the test folder for that application as a file.Index.js

```
var myApp = angular.module('myApp',[]);
myApp.controller('myController', function($scope) {
    $scope.ID =10;
});
```

The code creates an AngularJS module named myApp and defines a controller named myController. It assigns a variable named ID with a value of '10' to the scope object.

Create a test case that will verify if the code was properly executed.

Here is an example of a test code that can be used to verify the above code:

```
describe('myController', function() {
    beforeEach(module('myApp'));

    var $controller;

    beforeEach(inject(function(_$controller_) {
        $controller = _$controller_;
    }));

    describe('$scope.ID', function() {
        it('Check the scope object', function() {
            var $scope = {};
            var controller = $controller('myController', { $scope: $scope });
            expect($scope.ID).toEqual(10);
        });
    });
});
```

Key Points of the Test Code

beforeEach() function
This will load the Angular module named 'myApp' before executing the test.

The $controller object
This serves as a dummy object for "myController". This will be used to simulate the controller's behavior during testing.

beforeEach(inject(function(_$controller_)
This function will inject the dummy object.

var $scope = {};
This will serve as a dummy during testing and it is for the $scope object.

```
var controller = $controller('myController', { $scope: $scope });
```

This line will check if 'myController' exists and it will assign the variables from the controller's $scope object.

```
expect($scope.ID).toEqual(10);
```
This line compares $scope.ID to 10.

The test code will be stored in another file named ControllerTest.js. You can find this in the test folder.

CONCLUSION:

Thank you for downloading and reading this book. You have just learned a valuable web development tool that you can use to build highly responsive, dynamic, and exciting web pages. I hope that this special skill will help you achieve your personal and career objectives.

DID YOU ENJOY THIS BOOK?

We want to thank you for purchasing and reading this book. We really hope you got a lot out of it.

Can we ask a quick favor though?

If you enjoyed this book we would really appreciate it if you could leave us a positive review on Amazon.

We love getting feedback from our customers and reviews on Amazon really do make a difference. We read all my reviews and would really appreciate your thoughts.

Thanks so much.

iCode Academy

87190526R00101

Made in the USA
Lexington, KY
20 April 2018